The Certainty of the Unexpected

Pamela Ruth Stewart

The Certainty of the Unexpected

Onwards and Upwards Publishers

Berkeley House, 11 Nightingale Crescent, Leatherhead, Surrey, KT24 6PD.
www.onwardsandupwards.org

ISBN: 978-1-907509-58-2
Cover design: Leah-Maarit

Dedicated to

Mervyn

*Thank you for loving me
at my worst
and best*

*Your steady faith through great
personal suffering will inspire and
motivate me forever.*

See you in heaven...

Thank you...

...To Pastor Frank Parker for having a vision for this book before I did. I could never have done it without you; your spiritual guidance and standard of excellence enabled me to reach the finishing line!

...To Margaret Johnson for your generous and gracious support and being the golden link to my publisher.

...To all others who contributed and encouraged me along the way; you helped make this book a reality.

And finally,

...To my publishers, Onwards and Upwards Ltd, for enthusiastically taking on this project and prayerfully supporting its author.

Contents

Foreword

Pamela's book was inspired by the illuminating Biblical words of the Apostle Paul, recorded in Romans 8:28: "And we know that for those who love God *all things* work together for good; for those who are called according to His purpose." This principle governing the way of Christian life is not always easy to believe and accept, especially when things go wrong in life and mysterious tragedies occur which baffle human understanding and challenge the believer's faith in God. However it is precisely the resolution of this problem that miraculously emerges as the author's poignant yet triumphant story unfolds, demonstrating that the Christian believer can always experience the *certainty of the unexpected*.

It is a true and profoundly moving story, consisting of multiple themes like coloured threads expertly woven by the author, Pamela, into a deeply satisfying pattern. It is an exciting story describing the author's deliverance by God's grace from her entanglement since childhood in the bondage of a false cult. This was not an easy path to take. The book explains the problems involved when a cult member steps out from dark captivity into the sunshine of the liberty of the grace of God.

This book is a love-story. It reveals the intense love between husband and wife, the caring love of a daughter for her parents and the loyal love of a young Christian for her Lord – even when He allows her to suffer the hurt of losing her most precious treasure on earth.

My first encounter with Pamela's bright mind was several years ago when she was pursuing a Faith Mission Bible College correspondence course on Bible studies entitled 'Into the Word'. It was my privilege to mark her answers, and I soon discovered that she was a brilliant and diligent Bible student. She completed her course and was awarded her certificate with 'Distinction'.

I am, therefore, delighted to have the honour of highly recommending her book 'The Certainty of the Unexpected' to the general public readership. I am confident that this wonderful story will be a tremendous blessing to thousands of people and bring glory to the God of all grace.

Frank Parker
Apostolic Church Minister, Scotland
April 2012

No matter how many times
Our dreams are denied,
No matter how many times
We feel defeated or alone,

If we can stop and turn
Our hearts to Him
Who gave us life...

There will always be a way.

Anonymous

Chapter One

A Tragic Accident

Ecclesiastes 12:1 (ESV)
Remember also your Creator in the days of your youth

Tragedy

I will never forget the day that Annabel[1] was killed. There are days in life like that which are never forgotten, whether the reason is good or bad - days that stand out above all others; days when something happened that changed our lives for better or for worse. The day of Annabel's death changed my world from good to bad in an instant as I was made painfully aware of the fragile, unfair nature of life in this sin-stricken world. She shouldn't have died. She was too young. A freak, tragic accident had cut short the life of my ten-year-old friend with a shocking and bewildering finality. I was suddenly and brutally awakened to the harsh reality of life: bad things happen to good innocent people, even to children who are going about their ordinary routine in life.

We hear in the news of bad things happening, but for some reason, although we have sympathy, we relate to it in a different way when it has not been our own experience. How very different it is when tragedy happens to us personally. We can identify with strangers all over the world even though we do not know them. Although we cannot measure the depths of another's pain, we can understand the type of pain they are experiencing because it has been our own experience. I doubt that anyone can fully explain the type of pain that tragedy and bereavement bring. However, I do know that, once experienced, it leaves a life-time scar that time cannot erase. We wake in the mornings and go about our ordinary day not knowing what the day will bring forth. Things can suddenly change and leave us feeling numb with disbelief and desolation.

On the day of Annabel's death, I remember coming home from school to be greeted with that heart-stopping sentence: "I'm afraid I have very bad news to tell you."

How many times is that sentence used in a day, in a week, in a month, in a year as tragedies unfold all over the world? But in hindsight, how can any of us expect to live in such a troubled world and escape without having to deal with some kind of trauma, loss or grief?

It seems that on a bike-ride home from school, my friend had been in a terrible accident with a car and its trailer. What made the situation worse was that it had all happened on the road immediately outside her

---

[1] Name changed to protect identity.

front door. Even after all this time the memory can still make me shudder with horror.

Isn't it strange how in tragedies the "if only's" come hard and fast? *If only* the driver had been delayed for just a couple of minutes; it would have made the difference between life and death. *If only* Annabel hadn't gone to school that day. *If only* something had delayed her leaving school. "If only's" are endless. I have learned in life that they are like dead-end streets; they get you nowhere. Yet we still use them in grief, tragedy and loss. There is something within us that simply can't let go.

"If only's" made their appearance when our first ancestors, Adam and Eve, sinned against God in the Garden of Eden (or Paradise). I can only imagine the devastation and paralyzing regret they must have felt as they saw the terrible consequence of rebelling against God, as death and decay entered their perfect world. I wonder how many times they wept, saying "*If only* we hadn't listened to Satan's lies. *If only* we had talked to God about it first."

World's Best Preacher

I wept tears of sorrow and bewilderment as I stood at Annabel's grave and watched her casket lowered into the ground. I would never see her again. Her life had been tragically cut short. What if my life were to end so abruptly? It could have been me, and I was afraid - so afraid - of this horrible thing called death.

At thirteen years old I became terrified of dying and hated how helpless, hopeless and vulnerable it made me feel. I wept. Life suddenly seemed short and scary.

Sometimes I ask people whom they consider to be the world's best preacher. I find their answers to be very interesting. No one has ever given me the name of who I believe is the world's best preacher. I say his name is Death. You see, this preacher is so effective that he didn't need to say a single word to get my attention. There is no power on earth that can stop him preaching his distinctive message. There is no person who can argue or debate with this preacher. His voice may be silent, but it is louder than all other voices and has the final word. When we look at his ugly work, we are helpless to fix the problem and restore life again.

St Paul, the apostle, knew what he was talking about when he called death an enemy. An enemy does not work for our good. An enemy is there to defeat and destroy its target. Death is a devastating and inevitable experience that we will all have to face one day, sooner or later. But death is also my entrance into the glory of heaven because Jesus has saved me.

In the Biblical book of Hebrews, the writer tells us that Jesus Christ came to deliver those who were subject to lifelong fear of this enemy called death.

Hebrews 2:14-15

Because God's children are human beings – made of flesh and blood – the Son also became flesh and blood. For only as a human being could He die, and only by dying could He break the power of the devil who had the power of death. Only in this way could He set free all who have lived their lives as slaves to the fear of dying.

God, in His sovereign and infinite wisdom, allowed this 'enemy' to get my attention and wake me up to the reality and brevity of life. Life could end at any time, at any place, at any age. No one can be certain about the length of time each of us has here on this earth. It made me question the purpose of life. If this life is all we have then it simply does not make sense. What about people like Annabel who die young compared to others who live to be a hundred years old? Life must have a purpose, even if it is for a short time or a long time. That purpose must be to go on to something else after this life. If God allows such tragic things to happen then we must look for the larger plan He is working out from His standpoint of eternity.

Does He allow these things to happen because He sees how He can use them for our eternal good? Or does He allow these things to happen because He wants to see our responses and reactions? Will we turn to Him in our problems and pain, or will we turn away in bitterness and anger? The problem for us is that we work and look at things from an earthly perspective, and as a result we become discouraged and disillusioned.

Life with No Regrets

The scripture reading given at Annabel's grave was:

Ecclesiastes 12:1,7 (ESV)

Remember also your Creator in the days of your youth before the evil days come when you shall say I have no pleasure in them ... before the dust returns to the earth from where it came and the spirit returns to God who gave it.

As I listened to the reading, the words "remember ... your Creator" hit me straight away. It was as if someone had thumped me in the stomach and I was winded. The inner conviction that God was speaking to me, asking me to remember Him *now* was utterly astounding and powerfully convicting. If you have ever had that experience you will know that it is very special and powerful.

Maybe He will speak to you directly through the pages of this book. I am praying that He will. Anything is possible with God. He can use anything, even this book, to reach a seeking soul or crying heart that is searching for the answer and power to overcome our enemy called death.

I do know that when God speaks to us directly, He makes it clear so that there is no doubt. Today He speaks to us through His only begotten Son, Jesus Christ. If we want to know what God is like we are told to look to Jesus who is the image and exact representation of God. If we want to know what God expects from us we are told to listen to the words of Jesus and follow His example, clearly revealed in the Bible. Nothing and no one else is acceptable to God. It is the only way He has ordained for us to approach Him. That is why Jesus said:

John 14:6 (ESV)

I am the Way, the Truth and the Life, no one can come to the Father except through me.

Because we have a free choice we can choose either to respond to Jesus or to ignore Him. Jesus never imposes Himself on anyone. He simply waits and knocks gently on the door of our heart. I felt He was pleading with me to trust Him and let Him come in and live in my heart - not just for a day, a week, a month, a year, but forever.

I never had any indecision about accepting God and His son, Jesus Christ, into my life. I simply didn't want to die without their presence in my life. I wanted assurance that when I died I would be allowed into heaven. I was determined that from that time onward I would make sure this would happen. My sole purpose now would be to live to please God so that I would have no regrets at the end of my life.

A Surrendered Life

Tears flowed fast as I silently and willingly surrendered my life to God to use in whichever way He wished. Anyone looking at me would have assumed I was weeping purely because of Annabel, but my tears of bewilderment and loss were mingled with something else: shame. With a maturity beyond my years, I realized that without this tragedy I would not have thought of God or considered Him at all. There was no way I would have given Him any time or place in my plans for the future. I had been completely intent on what I was going to do and pleasing myself. However, the world's best preacher had changed all that. My ambitions and plans which had previously excluded God now suddenly disappeared. I knew that my life from now on would never be the same, but I believed that God could take the pieces of my life and work them together for my good in a different way beyond anything I could imagine.

The relief and peace that flooded my heart at that moment of surrender was awesome. There is nothing that can compare with knowing that your life is secure in God's hands. Where else can we find safety and security in a changing world of pain and sorrow? But I have discovered, since that first surrender, that surrendering to God is something that we continually have to do. There are constant challenges as our own wills battle against God's will in this sinful, materialistic, self-centred and hedonistic world.

I didn't understand much at that point in my life. I had never been to a Sunday school or been involved in any kind of Christian activity so my knowledge of the Bible was nil. Even though I had been brought up in a religious group that used the King James Version of the Bible there was no teaching or any kind of activity provided for children. We were required to sit still and be silent through every home meeting and every other missionary meeting in hired halls or rooms.

As a child I found those meetings to be a terrifying ordeal. The strained silence, the suffocating stillness and heavy atmosphere affected me deeply in a negative way. It was the perfect breeding ground for a phobia of religious meetings to develop. I used to feel like I was sitting in the middle of the reptile house at the zoo where all the different species would sit, immoveable, with cold, constantly staring eyes menacingly watching over me, just waiting for me to move a single muscle so that they could pounce upon me and say "I got you!" The suspense was crippling, and I felt as though I were waiting for the most awful bad news to be broken.

But despite all this, a tiny seed of faith was planted in my heart. I believed that I had been created for a purpose, and I just needed to find out what that was.

Day to be Remembered

Now there was another day that I would always remember. Who could forget the day when God speaks to them for the first time? It is etched on my mind forever. The sad day of Annabel's funeral was also a day when a new relationship began - a relationship with God Himself! I vowed to myself that Annabel's life would not be in vain. I decided that whenever I could I would tell others about her short life and the impact her death had had on me. I would share her life to make others think about the uncertainty of their own, so they could remember they had a Creator to whom we are all responsible before it is too late. Unbelievably, some good was now coming out of this terrible tragedy. I did not see it then, but looking back now I do.

For many years after Annabel's death I used to wonder what had happened to her. Had God taken her to heaven? We had never talked about such things. I worried about where she was. One day God gently showed me through His word that "Even a child is known by his acts" (Proverbs 20:11) and "Should not the Judge of all the earth do right?" (Genesis 18:25b). Things we don't understand can be left in the hands of a faithful Creator because the "Secret things belong to the Lord our God" (Deuteronomy 29:29, ESV). Jesus even said, "Not a single sparrow can fall to the ground without your Father knowing it. And the very hairs on your head are all numbered. So don't be afraid, you are more valuable to God than a whole flock of sparrows" (Matthew 10:29-31). I got so much peace from all this that I was able to leave her safely in God's hands. I knew that I could trust God with her. I didn't need to know the details.

First Spiritual Milestone

My first spiritual milestone is Annabel's grave - a place I try to visit once a year and remember where my journey with God began. It was at this place that the destiny of my life was changed. It is good to go back to our beginnings because we can look back through the years and see how faithful God has been through the ups and downs of life. Without fail, I always reflect with awe at His mercy in moving me out of a religion of works and fear to the Gospel (Gospel means good news) of grace and peace found only in Jesus Christ.

Spiritual milestones are important markers or memorials along life's journey. They can help consolidate our hopes and plans for the future. They remind us of God's goodness, graciousness and constant faithfulness despite our failures and shortcomings. They are important in times of discouragement and betrayal because they remind us that the same God who helped us through past traumas and difficulties is still there to help us through our present pain and problems. But most of all they are important because they remind us of a time when we experienced a momentous change:-

A change of heart
A change of mind
A change of purpose
A change of life
A change of priorities
A change of ambitions
A change of passion
A change of attitude

Very soon I was going to have the opportunity to make public the decision I had made at Annabel's funeral.

The Certainty of the Unexpected

Chapter Two

Religion's Hard Road

Proverbs 14:12
There is a way that seems right to a man,
but in the end it leads to death.

My Conversion

Life had now changed - inwardly rather than outwardly. I didn't feel able to discuss what had happened with anyone. People didn't talk very much about God outside of the meetings. I suppose it was just a follow on from the way the group leadership behaved. Everyone seemed very reserved about showing any kind of emotion or outward religious expression.

In fact, I wasn't sure if anyone would believe or even understand what I had experienced. But I did know the procedure that the preachers followed to allow people to make a decision to belong to God and the group; so that helped a little. I knew I would just have to wait for the right opportunity in one of the missionary meetings. I felt very anxious about having to wait. Several months later, however, I was given the opportunity to make my decision known in a public way. I had now turned fourteen years old.

As was the usual practice, the missionary meetings were held every spring and autumn in the area. These meetings took place in a mobile wooden unit positioned temporarily on local farmland. We called them Mission Huts. Inside the hut there was a partition at the far end where the two or three missionary workers had their sleeping quarters. I used to wonder how three people could fit in behind that screen; it must have been a squash. How would the others sleep if one of them snored?

There was a wood-burning stove positioned in the middle giving out plenty of heat and used for cooking and boiling water. I loved the smell of the burning wood. I liked to try and focus on these things. It took my mind away from that horrible, cold, hostile atmosphere that made me feel so uncomfortable. In one corner of the hut there was a small pedal organ which I found highly amusing. The person designated to play the hymns had to pedal away furiously to keep the sound coming out.

It was usual on the last night for an invitation to be given by the preachers for an opportunity to make 'a profession of faith'. The expression used then (and still today) was "Did anyone profess in your meetings tonight?" Or if they were wondering if someone belonged to the group they would ask, "Are they professing?"

As we travelled in the car to the meeting, my mother remarked that this was probably the last night. She wondered if anyone might profess. I remember thinking here was my opportunity at last! I went cold with fear and terror at the thought of having to stand up in front of everyone.

Apprehensively, I entered the mission hut. The tension was building up inside me. I wondered if I would have the courage to stand up. I have no idea what the two preachers said that night; I thought they would never finish! But eventually the senior missionary worker advised that if anyone would like to make a profession of their faith they should stand up when the last chorus of the final hymn was being sung.

My heart started pounding away furiously; it felt like a now-or-never moment. Somehow I had to do it! I had to make known the decision I had made of accepting God into my life.

The words of the last chorus sung were:

While the lamp of life is burning
And the heart of God is yearning
To His loving arms returning
Give thy wand'ring o'er.

At these words a sense of urgency filled my heart. It was only now that my lamp of life was burning; I could not be sure it would continue to burn even until tomorrow or next week, or next month, or next year. Annabel's death had made me realize the uncertainty of my own lifespan. It gave me the courage I needed. I jumped up like a big spring being released. I stood, shaking and sweating. I felt terribly self-conscious.

But then I felt a powerful, profound feeling of love surround me. I just knew that the words of the chorus applied to me personally; God really was yearning for me to turn and throw myself into His outstretched, loving arms. There was so much comfort in this experience that I was overwhelmed and burst into torrents of tears. Whoosh! It was like a dam bursting forth.

I felt an elbow nudge in my side. I realized that I was being warned to stop crying and it worked. My torrents of tears quickly turned into shuddering sobs. I was suddenly filled with the utmost amount of fear. I desperately tried to suppress myself, sitting down and shaking uncontrollably with the effort of trying to pull back my tears. Displays of emotional outbursts were not approved of in the meetings.

I remembered a conversation that some of the missionary workers had had at my parents' home. They had been discussing someone whose decision to 'profess' they had rejected. They had believed this person should wait until they were less emotionally charged. I did not want to find that I could not be accepted simply because I had burst into tears.

I was in a room surrounded by people, yet I suddenly felt alone and afraid. The crushing anxiety and fear that filled my heart at the thought of being rejected was crippling. It was just too awful to contemplate.

Soon the meeting came to an end. There was no reference made about the people who had stood up to show their decision to profess. As was the usual procedure, everyone silently filed out, shaking hands with one of the preachers on the way out. It was as if nothing had happened. Yet it had been a momentous occasion for me. I felt like a balloon that had suddenly been deflated. As I went through the door, the younger preacher whispered that he would come and visit me, but that was all.

I followed my parents as they walked to the car. Suddenly, one of the older girls ran across and hugged me. It was so unexpected that I had to fight back the tears once more.

A hug can mean more than a thousand words. It was something I never forgot; it meant such a lot to me at the time. I do this now in my chaplaincy work; there are times in tragic situations where a comforting hug is the only way to express sympathy.

Upon arrival home no one mentioned my tears, but I was pleased when my mother promised to get me a new Bible from Allan's, Publishers of Bibles in Scotland. She also told me that I could now take part in the home group fellowship meetings. And that was that.

It all seemed a terrible anti-climax. I felt drained at suppressing so much emotion, but at least I had accomplished what I had set out to do. Finally, I had let people know that I wanted God in my life.

However, that night in bed, instead of feeling joyful and relieved, I began to worry about what would now be expected of me. Would I be able to meet the required standards? I didn't feel very confident as I was shy and timid. The thought of speaking in the fellowship meetings filled me with dread. I had no clue about what to do or say about anything in the Bible or even how to pray out loud, though I knew everyone was expected to participate.

I had recently been given a small New Testament distributed by the Gideon's organization who had visited my school. It was a little burgundy coloured one which I had been so pleased to receive. I had a habit when anyone gave me a book of always checking the ending first. If the story ended in a happy way I would read it, but if the story finished with a sad ending I would refuse to read it.

I remember that my first Bible study took place at school in the playing fields. I sat my friends around me and bossed them into submission. They had to sit and listen to me read the last few chapters of the Bible: Revelations 20, 21 and 22. With eyes like saucers they heard about two destinations called heaven and hell.

At the end of the reading, one friend asked me whether I believed it was true or not. My response was "Of course it's true!" I told my friend that I was going to make sure I went to heaven when I died. My friends all agreed that they wanted to go to heaven too; it sounded so beautiful with no pain, suffering or death - nothing bad or evil could enter heaven.

We were all happy to read the Bible story because it had a beautiful ending if we went to heaven. We didn't like to think about hell or the final ending in the Lake of Fire. That seemed too awful. Yet we agreed that God was right and that bad, evil people and Satan shouldn't be allowed into heaven. They would spoil it for us.

This was my first attempt at teaching the Bible; it just seemed a natural thing to do. I loved it, although I am not sure that my friends did.

Fellowship Meetings

But it was very different in our fellowship meetings. The stiff atmosphere seemed to inhibit me and send me scurrying back into my shell.

The meetings took place on Sunday morning, Sunday evening and Wednesday evening. The first meeting that I could participate in was on Wednesday evening. The book of Psalms was currently being read, and Psalm 23 was the one that everyone was studying for on that night. Even though the meetings were organized in different homes, it was extremely formal and stiff. The format for the meeting was that people would come in through the unlocked front door, walk into the room with a nod of greeting and sit in silence until everyone else had arrived. It was normal practice for people to always sit in the same seat for each meeting. Once you sat in a seat no one else would sit there again. We were like homing pigeons - always returning to the same place or seat.

Usually the man of the house presided over the meeting. He was appointed as a 'Bishop' by the preachers. His role was to make sure everything and everyone was kept in order. He would choose a hymn out of our book, and someone would start the singing since we only ever sang a cappella (unaccompanied); then the rest of us would join in.

This used to cause me a great deal of amusement because if the person who had started the hymn pitched it too low then as we progressed through the verses the pitch would slide even lower so that everyone would be straining their vocal chords to try to reach the bottom notes. The opposite would happen if it was pitched too high; then people had to just shout or squeak to reach the top notes, and this was even more hysterically funny. Once I just burst out laughing, and everyone looked at me disapprovingly as if I had committed a terrible sin. In most homes there was a piano or keyboard, but they were not allowed to be used. When I queried why we couldn't use an instrument to help us, I was told it simply wasn't done and that we didn't want to be getting "like the world". It just didn't make sense to me, and as I loved music and playing the piano, it really frustrated and annoyed me. I thought it was nonsense.

After the first hymn chosen by the Bishop of the meeting, there was a time of prayer. Everyone took part, and usually we would kneel to pray. After this there was another hymn which anyone could choose, and then it was time for each person to speak, in no particular order, about the chapter we had all read. Finally, there was an opportunity to choose another closing hymn. When the meeting finished, there was some general chit-chat and occasionally a cup of tea before we all went home.

I had problems sleeping at night before my very first participation because I was so worried about what I should say. Psalm 23 started with "The Lord's my shepherd; I shall not want." When my time came in the meeting to speak, I just managed to blurt out that I was a lamb who loved Jesus. Jesus was now my loving shepherd, and I believed He would always care for me like a shepherd cares for and loves his lambs. That was all I could manage!

As for praying, I just listened carefully to the others and then copied in a parrot-like fashion. We prayed using the old King James style language. It felt strange and unnatural using the words 'thee', 'thou' and 'thy' as if I were an actor putting on a stage performance.

I was relieved to get my first meeting over, but I still had a great deal of questions, worries and concerns about things that I had read in the Bible. I was much too scared to ask any of the preachers; I didn't find them easy to approach. Even though we had many of the preachers living with us during a series of missionary meetings, they never offered to read or explain the Bible on an individual basis. It simply wasn't done.

Once, when I did become brave enough to ask questions, I was told that I needed to ask God for a revelation and that I should make sure I attended all the meetings as that was the best way to learn. It made me feel very inferior - as if I wasn't good enough yet for God to reveal anything to me. I wished that I had never asked.

One True Way

I also began to think about others who didn't belong to the true church. It seemed an awesome privilege to be brought up in a group that was the only true way left on the earth. We did not have a name to identify ourselves; we didn't need one. We were the continuation of the church that Jesus had set up in the Bible days. We referred to ourselves as the 'one true way'.

I felt sad that so many people didn't know about this and began to wonder if God wanted me to go out as one of the preachers when I was older. It seemed terrible to think that so many people were worshipping God in vain all over the world in buildings and congregations that our preachers condemned as heretical.

I had never been in a church building except through school when we visited the local church to sing some Christmas carols. The 'true church' (or 'body of people') always met in homes as they did in Bible days. I felt extremely guilty when I went inside the building and was glad when it was finished.

Our preachers had warned us never to get involved with any other church, group, denomination, organization, minister, pastor, theology or Bible training college. They were all condemned as false, and involvement might lead us astray from the true way that we followed, but I felt sad that if I ever got married it would not be in a church building. This church had been really impressive inside. I day-dreamed about it; it would be so special to walk down that beautiful aisle in a flowing bridal gown to a wonderful man waiting for me at the end, but that kind of thought was sinful. I rebuked myself for even thinking that way.

Homeless Unmarried Preacher

I thought about becoming a preacher. I thought about what I would have to renounce. I wanted to help others, and I wanted to give my best to God, but I knew that it was a very high standard that I would need to maintain. I would have to give up any thought of getting married.

Our preachers had to remain single. Preachers who met someone they fell in love with and wanted to marry had to leave the mission field. The leaders were very strict about this. I knew someone who offered himself to be a homeless preacher, but when they found out that he had a girlfriend he had to finish the relationship. It seemed a really hard and unloving attitude to me, particularly when God had ordained marriage in the first place. It was also confusing. Most of the disciples and apostles of Jesus had been married.

When I queried the fact that the apostle Paul had written that "forbidding marriage is among the doctrine of devils" (1 Timothy 4:1-3), I was told by a senior preacher that they did not actually *forbid* marriage. Instead he said that being single was something they felt worked better. When prospective preachers thought about it, they came to the same conclusion. I was now totally confused and perplexed - they had a rule in practice but not in theory; how contradictory was that!

I would also have had to give up the right to have my own home, income or possessions. We claimed to follow the way Jesus sent His Apostles out to preach:

Matthew 10:5-15

Don't go to the Gentiles or the Samaritans, but only to the people of Israel – God's lost sheep. Go and announce to them that the Kingdom of Heaven is near. Heal the sick, raise the dead, cure those with leprosy, and cast out demons. Give as freely as you have received. Don't take any money in your money belts, no gold, silver, or even copper coins. Don't carry a traveller's bag with a change of clothes and sandals or even a walking stick. Don't hesitate to accept hospitality, because those who work deserve to be fed.

Similar verses are found in Luke 10:1-10. No-one in the whole world was prepared to follow this criterion the way we did. I thought it was very impressive. However, I didn't understand why no one prayed for the sick or cast out demons.

It was only later on that I discovered that the 'one true way' religion had been started by a Scotsman named William Irvine (1863-1947). He was born in Newtown, Kilsyth, Scotland and died in Jerusalem. He was converted to Christ through the preaching of Presbyterian evangelist Rev. John McNeil in Motherwell and in 1895 joined the Faith Mission as an evangelical pilgrim. In 1896 he was sent to Southern Ireland as a pilgrim preacher to work at Menagh, County Tipperary. Whilst working there, Irvine claimed to have received a special revelation of Matthew 10:5-15. He claimed that 'true' preachers should renounce all possessions, marriage, job, income or wage and become homeless - although they could live in members' homes. He failed to identify that this specific message was for the 12 Jewish Apostles at that time in Israel's history and that some of them were also married and had homes! Nor did he realise that these instructions were reversed by Christ just before his crucifixion in Luke 22:35-36.

In 1901, when Irvine resigned officially from the Faith Mission, a warning was placed in 'Bright Words' (the official periodical of the Faith Mission at that time) concerning a new sect that was being formed by Irvine.

Of course, I was completely unaware of the founder's erroneous interpretation; I had simply accepted all that I had been taught from childhood. I liked the thought of being a travelling preacher, but I realised that money could be a problem. 'Homeless' preachers had to rely on members to support them financially, but this was where going out by faith in God became real. I had heard preachers say that it all depended upon how much faith you had in God to meet your needs from day to day.

I really thought very seriously about following their example. I admired the 'homeless' preachers for the great sacrifice they had made in giving up so much for God. I saw that there was a great need for more preachers like this because people could only come to Jesus and be saved for eternity through a homeless preacher. They would also have to conform to the lifestyle of asceticism that the homeless preachers had instituted.

An Ascetic Lifestyle

We did not have televisions, radios, hi-fi music systems, or any such items in our homes; they were considered evil and worldly. It was really difficult at school. I never told anyone, but when others were talking about TV programmes it was evident that I didn't have a clue what they were referring to. It was also hard if we had to go on school trips because of the rule we had that females should not wear trousers. To be the only female wearing a skirt was humiliating. My mother eventually took pity on me and bought me a pair of trousers so that I could go on a special school walking trip. It was such a relief. Sometimes I would cry my eyes out because I felt so excluded and embarrassed at being the odd one out in the class. When it became too much I would just disappear to avoid these situations.

I hated school. It was so hard to concentrate in class. I was always so tired after attending the missionary meetings in the evenings. The strained atmosphere always sapped my energy, but I seemed to come alive in the English and Music classes. I loved those subjects. I would lose myself in an imaginary world of words and beautiful sounds. I even joined the guitar group at high school; it opened up a whole new world of songs and music styles, the like of which I had never heard before. The rhythms were exciting and fun - nothing like the dreary hymns we were forced to sing in our meetings. I was invited to sing a solo with a boy who was a fabulous accompanist on the guitar at the Christmas Concert. I thought it so ironic that the song I was asked to sing was "There are no lights on our Christmas tree; we must not spoil the tel-ee-vee (television!)" But it was a fantastic experience and I loved every minute of it. I wished the homeless preachers would allow things like that in our meetings.

I had now reached the age where hair had become an issue. Conformity in hairstyles for females was an important part of the true way church doctrine. We were expected to follow the advice that the apostle Paul gave: that a woman should have long hair because it was her glory (1 Corinthians 11:15).

Due to this, females were expected to have long hair tied back until they got older and then put up in a bun or roll on top their head. My hair was straight and smooth; when I left school it was hard to wear it in a bun because if I moved too much it would all fall down or sit lopsided on my head. I had to have so many of those huge hairgrips in my head to try to keep it in place that I felt like a metal hedgehog.

I have lost count of the many hours I would often spend fussing about my hair; at times I would cry with despair as I found it such hard work. Sometimes people would call us the bun-head religion because of the uniform hairstyle amongst the females.

I envied the girls who wore make-up; that was banned for us too. I also loved the jewellery they wore - fancy, colourful necklaces and earrings of all kinds of shapes and styles - but extravagances such as that were strictly prohibited. In fact, only wedding bands were allowed; even engagement rings were forbidden.

It was a very austere and narrow-minded existence, but I accepted it even if it upset me because I believed what the preachers taught: that these things all displeased God. Some of the female homeless preachers were exceedingly strict. One girl was sent out of the meeting because she was wearing white shoes which they considered looked too worldly. We were supposed to be different from the world in how we dressed and looked.

We were also supposed to avoid 'worldly places' and activities. We would never set foot in a pub, get involved in card-games, gambling and bingo, visit the cinema, theatre, dance halls or funfair parks; these kind of places were strictly out of bounds. In any case, I was so busy going to all the meetings that there would not have been time for such things anyway.

Baptism

I had been waiting to be told when I could be baptized, and when approval was given I was thrilled. I hoped that once this happened I would start to feel different - happier and fulfilled.

To be water baptized meant you had to be fully immersed in water. Jesus submitted to baptism, not because He had sins to repent of, but because He wanted us to follow His example (Matthew 3:13-17). It was a symbol of washing away the sins of our old life or dying to our old life of sin and rising up out of the waters to a new life of holiness before God.

My baptism took place on farmland where there was a clean stream of running water with a depth that reached well over my waist. I had to dress in old clothes. On top I wore an old coat several sizes too big for me and held together at the bottom with large safety pins. On my head I wore a tight rubber bathing cap to keep my hair dry. A strange sight indeed, but I really didn't care at all how I looked; I just wanted so much to be baptized.

It would have been great to have had some applause when I came up out of the water but there was nothing. The people who watched were still and silent as was expected on such occasions. I wished that someone would cheer and shout with joy. I was becoming so tired of all this stiff, cold formality. I wondered what God was thinking as He looked down at me. Did He have something special in life that I could do for Him, I wondered? I felt quite emotional; my baptism was a very personal commitment to God. I prayed with all my heart that he would use my life in an extraordinary way.

I looked up at the blue sky and hoped the Holy Spirit would come down and settle on me like a dove - just the way it had happened to Jesus when He came up out of the water (Matthew 3:16). He didn't though. I was so disappointed, but still I knew something significant was happening. I cannot explain it, but I knew that God had heard my request and would one day answer it.

Getting out was worse than getting in as water-logged clothes weighed me down, although there were helping hands to pull me up out of the water. I walked back to the changing hut, my shoes making the most awful squelching, sucking sound across the grass. Funny, the insignificant things you can remember at significant times! But I was glad I had done it. I felt as though I had achieved something very special in copying the example of Jesus.

Heart's Frustrated Desire

Despite all this, I remained frustrated and unhappy. Something was missing, but I could not work out what it was. I tried so hard to conform to everything that was required - to keep the exacting standards of lifestyle and behaviour - but it didn't give me any joy, peace or satisfaction. I felt heavy and weighed down with the burden of it all. From the beginning of my relationship with God it had been my heart's desire to let God use my life for some special purpose, but there was a deep sense of anticlimax to everything.

The most miserable thing of all was the strange sensation that came over me in every meeting; that 'reptile house' atmosphere seemed to be growing out of proportion. Whether it was a missionary meeting or a home meeting, the atmosphere was weird and heavy as if something were in the room. I tried so hard to ignore it and pretend I was satisfied and happy, but inside I was totally freaked out. Worse still was the feeling of shame and guilt that I should feel like this, and I started to wonder what was wrong with me or even if God was angry with me for some reason. Year after year the tension and pressure inside me kept building up and up.

Again I thought seriously about forsaking everything to become one of the group's missionary workers, but I realised that I had to overcome this strange reaction and awareness. How could I go and preach convincingly to others when I was so miserable and uncertain myself?

Once a year it was usual for rally calls to be made for the young people to forsake everything to become missionary workers. The challenge was to "sacrifice everything for Jesus". This type of call would normally take place at the annual conventions held during the summer months. Several hundred people would gather for a four day convention of meetings up and down the UK. Preachers from all over the world would attend these gatherings.

I always felt as though they would never end, but there was no way I could get out of attending. It was a compulsory thing to do. I had to sit and pretend I was enjoying it like everyone else appeared to be doing. It was indescribable torture to sit still through each meeting; I just wanted to run as fast as I could, away from it all. The constant, dreary drone of speakers was like buzzing mosquitoes constantly whirring around my head while I spiralled down and down into despair.

A Terrible Secret

When the rallying calls were made, encouraging the young people to sacrifice everything for Jesus, I knew I would be unable to fulfil that calling. I felt ashamed as I saw others give their lives to work in the mission field. In comparison, my own future looked bleak and desolate. I felt God viewed me as a hopeless case.

Finally, I reached the point where I had to admit that this 'faith' just wasn't working in my life, no matter how hard I tried. The guilt of feeling such a terrible, evil presence in the meetings weighed heavy on my young shoulders, but it was so real to me that I found it hard to understand why no one else noticed it. I did everything I could to hide my 'terrible' secret. How could I discuss this strange experience I was having with anyone? No one would understand and, worse still, they might even excommunicate me. This was a very lonely and perplexing experience; it just didn't make sense.

At the time I didn't understand that God had given me the gift of discerning the presence of a false spirit at work - an influence that distorts Scripture and deceives people to believe and trust in something that God never intended.

A Desperate Prayer

I contemplated my future. It didn't look promising, and tears were shed most nights. How much longer could I keep up this pretence? Fear gripped me inside like an ever-tightening band. I wondered if I would be able to survive another twelve months, never mind twelve years. Outside, people around me had no clue as to what was going on inside.

One night, in desperation, I pulled back the curtains of my bedroom window and silently shouted, "God, if you really are a God who answers prayer, will you please help me? Show me what it is you want me to do; show me what is missing. I just have no strength left to pretend anymore."

For some reason I hadn't really cried out to God with such desperation before. Like a bolt of lightning hitting me, I suddenly realised that because I had felt guilty about my reactions, I had even been trying to hide my pain and confusion from God! How foolish was that! He was there to help me, not to ridicule me. I also realised that the unsympathetic attitude of the preachers towards anyone who had doubts was one that I had assumed God would have also. Even if I shared my experiences with them now after all these years I would not be surprised if they looked at me disbelievingly and unsympathetically.

This revelation came as I was staring at a full moon. In its fullness it just looked so beautiful, peaceful and serene. It was the complete opposite of my mental state, and I envied it. Suddenly everything seemed surreal because, despite my agony of mind, I felt a peace flow through me that was indescribable. I got back into bed and I slept. There was none of the usual anxious tossing and turning that night. These days, whenever I look at a full moon it reminds me of that night.

Psalm 102:19-20

From heaven the Lord looked at the earth, to hear the groans of the prisoners, to set free those who were doomed to die.

Psalm 66:18-20

If I had cherished sin in my heart, the Lord would not have listened. But truly God has listened: He attended to the voice of my prayer. Blessed be God, because He has not rejected my prayers or removed His steadfast love from me!

Little did I know how wonderfully God was going to answer my prayer beyond anything I could ever have hoped or dreamed.

The Certainty of the Unexpected

Chapter Three

Good News Called Grace

Ephesians 2:8

*God saved you by His grace when you believed. And you
can't take credit for this, it is a gift from God.*

The Gift of a Person

It wasn't long before I met the answer to my prayer, although I did not know it at the time. In a million years I could never have imagined the extraordinary effect of such an ordinary meeting.

Sometimes God answers our prayers in ways far beyond that which we could ever ask or think. I didn't pray to God for someone special to come into my life to help me; I prayed for guidance. I didn't pray for marriage; I prayed to be shown what to do. I didn't pray for a new life; I asked for strength to endure the one I had. God answered my prayer abundantly. All the things I asked for and more were wrapped up in the gift of a person - Mervyn - who became my husband.

I don't think any of us can estimate the powerful impact that one solitary life can have on another. God can use just one life to change our lives completely for an eternal purpose. God was able to use Mervyn's life to impact me. This was because he had submitted and surrendered his will and life to God. It proves that when we let God work freely in our lives, He can then use us to reach out and help others through life's difficulties and traumas - probably in ways we could never have dreamed of or imagined.

I love the quote "When God wraps a gift, He wraps it in a person."[2] Gifts can be unwrapped immediately, but they can also be unwrapped slowly and carefully over a period of time. There are times when we can recognize immediately that God has sent someone to help us, but there are also times when it takes a little while to work out that a particular person is the answer to our need.

At our first meeting I had no idea of the future, life-changing impact that would result; nor did I suspect that we would be married several years later! At the time it was the last thing on my mind. Members of the 'true way' church were not encouraged to marry or get involved with anyone outside of the group.

I left school at sixteen years of age. I had the opportunity to take a job as trainee Junior Secretary. This included a study day and evening every week at a local college. Over the next three years I decided to work

---

[2] William Lane – 'The Walk" by Michael Card, Discovery House Publishers

towards a Private Secretary's Diploma. But my heart wasn't really in this decision. I didn't find it fulfilling in a personal way.

I thought I could train as a nurse instead. I liked comforting people and making them feel better, but one of the strict female homeless preachers made it quite clear that working shifts meant I would miss my appointments with God in the meetings. Looking back now it is fascinating to see the way God has opened the door for me to become a part-time member of a Hospital Chaplaincy team. The comforting streak that was in me at an early age is fully utilized in that role. However, at the time I decided that it didn't really matter what I did. It would only be temporary. My heart's desire was that one day I would be a missionary preacher.

I met Mervyn six months after my prayer of desperation. I had moved to my second job as a Sales and Marketing Secretary. He arrived from Northern Ireland to take up a new management position at the company where I was employed in the North West of England. He literally turned up in front of my desk, asking if he could borrow my rubber!

He was very tall with large, expressive green eyes and the manners of a gentleman. I was struck by how warm and kind his eyes were; there was nothing cold or judgmental in their expression. However, his sense of humour could be wicked. After borrowing my rubber, he then asked for my ruler; after my ruler he asked for a paper-clip; after a paper-clip he asked for an envelope. By this time I was getting frustrated as I was trying to concentrate on a report that needed to be finished. When he next asked for my stapler, I slammed it down on the desk and pointedly ignored him.

To my consternation he simply burst out laughing and wandered off without using it. I suddenly realized he had been teasing me all along and I had fallen for it.

I Need a Good Meal!

Our first meeting had an unusual effect on Mervyn. He perceived a light glowing around me and immediately discerned that God was highlighting me out to him for a specific reason. Instinctively, he perceived an inner struggle of a spiritual nature. He also thought, "Oh, no, what's wrong with her? She looks like she needs a good meal!" In his eyes, I looked haunted, pale and agitated. It was certainly not a romantic start!

As I got to know Mervyn, he started to send what he called "survival packs" through the internal company post or leave large packages on my desk. They contained sandwiches with all kinds of fillings. There were also fruit juice cartons, nutritional bars, Wagon Wheels, Kit Kats (his favourite) and apples and oranges. The idea, apparently, was to build me up.

At first I did not know quite what to make of this approach. It was unusual to say the least, but I did find it quite amusing and filling! I would munch happily away through it all during the day.

Our paths began to cross in the workplace, and we started to have interesting discussions. I remember one discussion in particular: Mervyn told me about an incident that had had a powerful influence on his life when he was a teenager. A family friend, a man who was an atheist, had found his wife reading the Bible. In his fury, he had grabbed her Bible and had thrown it onto the open fire. Immediately the hand that had thrown it shrivelled up and became useless. This incident instilled in Mervyn a deep reverence and respect of both the Scriptures and the Bible's author (God) because "All scripture is inspired by God" (2 Timothy 3:16). Mervyn never had any doubts about the Bible being inspired by God, but then neither did I. Apparently, neither did the atheist! Unsurprisingly, that experience turned him into an immediate believer!

Mervyn had become a Christian when he was seven years old. I was astounded. Our preachers would say it was too young an age to know what it all meant. As a child I would not have been allowed (or even encouraged) to make such an important decision, yet Mervyn's faith as a Christian had been grounded in him as a child. He described attending a local Faith Mission outreach meeting with his family when he was seven years old.

That night, at the end of the meeting, the Faith Mission Worker had challenged everyone with the question, "Are you ready for eternity? Have you asked Jesus Christ to save you from your sins? If you were to die tonight, have you made your peace with God through Jesus?"

It affected Mervyn deeply. He couldn't sleep that night and went to wake up his father. In tears he told his father he wanted to be ready to meet God when he died. He wanted to make sure his sins were forgiven before he could fall asleep. In the middle of the night they both knelt down at the bedside as Mervyn asked Jesus into his heart and life:

Father God,
I know that I am a sinner and need forgiveness.
I believe that Jesus died for my sins.
I want to turn from my sins (repent).
I now invite Jesus to come into my heart and life.
Help me to trust and follow Jesus as long as I live.
In Jesus' name. Amen.

After that prayer, Mervyn slept soundly. He had made his peace with God through Jesus. Now he wasn't afraid to die; at seven years old he knew he was ready to meet God.

I had never heard anything so astonishing. I didn't think I was a sinner or a bad person. It didn't seem logical or relevant to someone who belonged to the only true church; or had I missed something? I began to feel a bit uneasy. I was also envious. I did not possess such assurance.

The Gospel (or Good News) of Grace

A new series of missionary meetings began in the local area. I gave Mervyn an invitation card. He had been asking when the meetings would be held and also how the 'true way' group was structured.

I found it embarrassing when I had to say I couldn't take him to the meetings. I knew there would be backchat if a single woman accompanied a man who was not a member of our group. It created a lot of unwelcome gossip, even if it was just a friendship. Having a relationship with anyone outside the group was frowned upon. I began to realise that the group had a very narrow-minded attitude.

The meetings were held in a hired room of a local school. I wondered what Mervyn would make of the stiff atmosphere. There were normally two preachers speaking - an older person and a younger trainee person. We either had two male preachers or two female preachers. We had been nicknamed 'the two-by-twos' due to the way that the preachers always travelled together in twos; this was following the pattern Jesus had used when He sent out His first disciples "two by two" (Luke 10:1).

The message that night was the same as usual. If there was an outsider present, the preacher would emphasise the one 'true way' on the earth: people could only be accepted by God if they came to Jesus through the preaching of our homeless preachers and conformed to the 'true way' lifestyle of asceticism. I remember particularly the younger preacher speaking of his concern for the future: what if the sacrifice of the preachers to give up everything (a home, career and marriage) for the sake of the Gospel didn't continue; what would happen to the 'true way' then?

The meeting was more solemn and gloomy than usual. Afterwards we all filed silently out after a goodnight handshake at the door.

Nothing prepared me for Mervyn's reaction. I had thought he would be impressed; instead he was utterly devastated! He was deeply concerned that the Gospel Message (Good News) of God's grace towards us through Jesus was obviously not understood or presented. It was a false message.

If I had been hit on the head I couldn't have been more surprised or thrown off balance. I could not understand what he was talking about. I had thought grace meant a special quality we had to have in our lives. I remembered vividly one of our preachers saying grace was like oil: as oil was used to make things run smoother so we all needed more grace to get on with each other better.

Mervyn challenged me to think about the bad news first.

Romans 3:23

For everyone has sinned, we all fall short of God's glorious standard.

No one can attain the standard of perfection God requires. Sin has entered the human race through the disobedience of the first created man and woman. As a result, no-one who has ever lived is able to say he or she has:

Never done anything wrong
Never thought anything wrong
Never said anything wrong

The 'Good News' (Gospel) was that God, in His infinite grace (mercy and love), sent Jesus to take the punishment for all sin! Jesus died on the cross to pay the penalty for our sins. The death of Jesus on the cross is the reason why we can receive forgiveness.

Romans 6:23

For the wages of sin is death, but the free gift of God is eternal life through Jesus Christ our Lord.

That is why it is unacceptable if we put our faith in:

A denomination

A renunciation of possessions, marriage or money

A church membership or institution

A religious system or exclusive group

A religious education

A doctorate in theology or degree

A special experience or vision

A charitable work

A personal feeling

A priest, minister or pastor

A homeless preacher

God asks us to put our faith in His Son, Jesus. Jesus is the person who has done all that is necessary to secure our acceptance by God.

Finding God's Amazing Grace in Jesus

I was challenged to read:

Ephesians 2:8-10

God saved you by his grace when you believed. And you can't take credit for this; it is a gift from God. Salvation is not a reward for the good things we have done, so none of us can boast about it. For we are God's masterpiece. He has created us anew in Christ Jesus, so we can do the good things he planned for us long ago.

God in His grace gives us an unmerited gift of eternal life through faith in Jesus. This means God offers us a guarantee of heaven, not because of what we have done but because of our faith in Jesus. Without faith in Jesus we can never be acceptable to God; we can never enter heaven and have eternal life.

I didn't have to approach God through a homeless preacher, a minister, a pope, a priest or any other religious figure or person; the only acceptable way to approach God was directly through Jesus. A true minister, priest or teacher would point people to Jesus not themselves, their own sacrifices or efforts. Jesus would transform my life and help me live in a way that pleased God.

Titus 2:11-12

For the grace of God that bringeth salvation hath appeared to all men. Teaching us that denying ungodliness and worldly lusts, we should live soberly, righteously, and godly, in this present world.

We seek to live a godly life as a response to his grace: His undeserved favour towards us.

I felt a cold hand of fear grip my heart tightly. A powerful conviction had come over me as I listened, but I did not want to examine my reaction. It was simply too scary. No, it was unthinkable! Surely there was nothing wrong with what I believed... or was there? I found myself desperately reiterating the need for a homeless preacher, the church in a home and an ascetic lifestyle. I was like a mechanical doll reciting a recorded message. It felt hollow and unsubstantial.

An Earth Tremor

My world seemed to be shaking as though I was on the threshold of a profound breakthrough, but then something strange happened. I felt an inner power rising up and taking control over my thoughts. However hard I tried to think about what Mervyn had presented, my mind rejected it as if it were an unwelcome distraction.

The only way I can describe this violent reaction is comparing it to an emergency stop in a car driving test. The requirement was to slam the brakes on in order to stop immediately. I discovered my mind could do the same. It would slam into stop mode. Worse still, it made me adopt a defensive and intransigent attitude. This can be a typical response from a person who has been indoctrinated.

The grace of God offered to me in Jesus seemed unbelievably easy. That made me feel it was wrong. I was used to feeling weary, oppressed and heavily burdened with my religion.

I thought of the invitation Jesus offered:

Matthew 11:28-30
Come to me, all of you who are weary and carry heavy burdens, and I will give you rest. Take my yoke upon you. Let me teach you, because I am humble and gentle at heart and you will find rest for your souls. For my yoke is easy to bear and the burden I give you is light.

This picture of rest and simplicity seemed beyond me. Would I ever be able to break free from the stronghold that held me captive and burdened? What would it take to find the delete key? Where would I find the strength to break free from the chains that bound me?

The Certainty of the Unexpected

Chapter Four

Setting the Captive Free

Matthew 11:28

Come to me, all of you who are weary and carry heavy burdens, and I will give you rest.

Finding the Delete Key

The Bible speaks of those who hold false opinions or beliefs as being held captive by Satan (2 Tim 2:26). My mind had been held under a powerful influence since childhood. It would be a fierce battle to break free.

Mervyn compared it to a computer program. No matter how many keys he pressed, I just wouldn't respond differently. The 'true way' group setting had to be deleted. Only then would I be free to accept or consider new information.

I was unhappy. Very reluctantly, I had declined a dinner date with Mervyn. It had been a struggle to say no and keep to the rules. I hated it. I felt as though I had lost someone really special. He was such good company and fun. I could be myself with him, which seemed an odd thing under the circumstances. I didn't like how pretentious I had become. It shocked me. It was as though I was trying to act out another character in order to please the 'true way' manner of living.

Mervyn hid his disappointment behind a joking manner. He teased me about all I would be missing and left the invitation open. He hoped that I would change my mind. Fortunately he wasn't a person to give up at the first or second hurdle though. His faith was strong, and he knew God had His hand on our relationship. God's plan and purpose would not be thwarted despite any setbacks. Mervyn could wait and he could pray. In time, he believed, my life would be used to glorify God's amazing grace and mercy.

I was to be surprised at the next move. Mervyn sent me a single, exotic, fresh orchid on Valentine's Day. It was breathtakingly beautiful. I was amazed at the words he had written on the card:

Much has been written on Orchids
And most of it's probably true,
But just two words that describe them best
Apply just as much to you.
"Rare and Beautiful"

One day, I hope you will be my wife!

I was stunned at such an unusual proposal. I didn't quite see myself like an exotic orchid either! Maybe eating all the survival packs of food he had sent had paid off! However, we agreed to take things slowly as I was struggling with my situation.

The oppressive atmosphere in the 'true way' meetings was getting progressively worse. I felt like a hamster going round and round on a treadmill. I wanted to get off but didn't know how to stop it. I began to despair again. When would the promised answer to my desperate prayer for help appear?

I changed jobs once more and began working as a Director's PA at another company so I saw less of Mervyn. I was surprised by how much I missed him. Then one night something snapped; I would make my own decisions about personal matters! I let Mervyn know I had changed my mind, and we began to spend a lot of time together.

Mervyn had now become a close friend of one of the male homeless preachers. I was amazed to see this friendship grow, and they became very close, reading the Bible together and sharing thoughts. But, tragically, this homeless preacher became terminally ill. Mervyn was utterly devastated. He began praying for a healing miracle, but the 'Way' group had no time for this and he was ridiculed. They believed the gifts of the early church no longer existed.

It opened my eyes. Prayer for the sick was the advice given in the Bible! (James 5:14). It is also a natural expression of outward concern when you care about someone, but the leadership did not believe in praying in this manner. I found this attitude incomprehensible.

I was to have another shock. I was surprised to learn the preacher's nursing care was paid from the group's funds. I hadn't known they had any. I had always believed the group had no funds or bank accounts. It seemed they had no open and transparent policy with regard to financial matters. Such clandestine arrangements left me feeling very uncomfortable and uneasy.

I began to see two very different worlds colliding in beliefs and attitudes, but to question anything was very difficult. Fear and conformity had been indoctrinated in me as a child. I hadn't realized how much I was controlled by it; it had made me passive and weak. It would be a tough battle to stand alone and voice any concerns.

There was an even greater fear. Anyone who left the group would not be accepted by God when they died. Hell would be their destination. This belief was a very powerful stronghold in my life. I suppose it kept a lot of people from leaving the group. It was equally terrifying to consider that anything I had been taught was false. It seemed too awful to contemplate.

I hid my unease and concern by being defensive towards Mervyn's belief in God's saving grace through faith in Jesus. How could so many good living people be wrong? My mind slammed into shut-down mode.

Breaking the Mould

However, my defensive attitude was cut short. Startled, I noticed tears running down Mervyn's cheeks. I was stunned into silence. To see such raw pain at my unreasonable reaction was awful. An enormous shockwave of shame roared through me. It was so powerful - like being hit by a bolt of lightning.

But then something awesome happened. Instantly, I felt a deep release from within my mind as the 'override switch' smashed into smithereens. A power over me had been broken, as if heavy chains had fallen off. I was free! My mind would never slam into shut-down mode again.

What an incredible experience - my intransigent setting deleted forever, never to return again! From that moment, I was able to listen, reason and discuss without shutdown mode taking over.

My heart goes out to people held under the bondage of indoctrination. They may long to break free but feel they can't. I pray this book will help them realise they can. Nothing is impossible with God!

This experience freed me in other ways as well. For the first time, I felt able to share with Mervyn my inner trauma - how I felt an evil presence or influence in the group's meetings. It did not make sense to me since outwardly everything looked normal and good. But Mervyn was not surprised. It seems he had already sensed my discomfort in the meetings. He believed I had an ability or gift - sensitivity to evil spiritual influences. It was like having a sensory device that bleeps to alert something is seriously wrong. I had not had the spiritual understanding to discern what was happening. Instead I had simply blamed myself.

I was truly stunned. I just sat and stared like I was in a dream. All these years I had believed I was the problem. He was telling me that it was the group's teaching that was the problem. I was completely overwhelmed as indescribable relief flooded through me. Suddenly my world had completely changed. This huge burden I had carried around for so long just fell off my shoulders. It was like a boulder suddenly rolling off the edge of a cliff-top.

Despite this experience though, I felt that I had no alternative but to remain in the group. I did not want to upset my family as my parents would be devastated if I left. They would never understand my spiritual agony. It would be beyond them.

As I discussed all this with Mervyn, I suddenly realised that God had given me a person who loved me despite all of my problems and difficulties. A bright, illuminating light had suddenly been switched on. It was the moment I knew I loved him.

Why had it taken me so long to realise this? It really was true that "when God wraps a gift, He wraps it in a person" I had been given a very special gift. But it had taken several years to unwrap it! God had answered my desperate prayer in a way beyond all I had ever dreamed or imagined.

Here is a poem Mervyn wrote on a picture card which says it all:

Dear Pamela

You'll know who this reminds me of,
One I've loved so long,
One that I gave my heart to,
One who makes me strong.
One who lights my darkness
And helps me now to see,
The depth and power contained in love
Means future hope for me.

One who's always in my thoughts,
Even when far away,
Filling my mind, assuring me
Our time will come, some day.
Helping me plan the future,
Knowing of doubts and fears,
Learning to overcome through love,
Learning to dry the tears.

Trusting in one another
Even in times of doubt,
Knowing each other's weaknesses,
This is what love's about.
Sharing each new experience,
Journeying side by side,
Strengthening the invisible bond,
Willingness to confide.

These are a few of my thoughts today,
Things that I hope we'll do,
But I know that I'll only be happy
If my future is shared with you.

There was nothing I wanted more than to share my life with Mervyn. God had chosen to bring him into my life in answer to my desperate prayer. How could I not trust God with the future now, whatever it might hold?

Wedding Day

I have another special day to remember.

From the first day we met to our wedding day was exactly six years. I had never felt so happy even though I didn't get my dream of walking down an aisle in a beautiful church. Members of the group would never consider using a church building for a wedding ceremony. It was usually a Registry Office or whatever other local venue could be used at the time.

I know this disappointed Mervyn. I felt very bad about the compromise he was making; he would have loved traditional hymns and a formal church ceremony.

However, we both acknowledged that it wasn't all about the external things. It was about making a personal commitment and vow to each other before God. The place was secondary. When I said, "'till death do us part" in the ceremony, I silently winged a special prayer request to God. I wanted us both to die together. I didn't want to be left a widow. It would be unbearable. God had brought us together in a remarkable way. He was more than capable of arranging what I wanted - or so I hoped.

I decided that the present was too special to be overly concerned about such things as dying! After the wedding we initially spent a few days in the Lake District. Our official honeymoon took place a few weeks later when we jetted off on a fly/drive tour of Israel Kibbutz's. It was a phenomenal, once-in-a-lifetime experience.

Scales Fall Off My Eyes (Dr Billy Graham Sermon!)

Mervyn never once put any kind of pressure on me to leave the group. He just wanted me to fully realize and experience joy in the concept of God's saving grace in Jesus. However, he was concerned about the negative effect the meetings were having on me in a physical, emotional and spiritual way - but things were about to change dramatically.

A Christian outreach evening was being held in the local theatre. It was an event organized by different churches. The highlight of the evening would be a sermon by video relay. The preacher was an American man named Dr. Billy Graham. Mervyn was really keen to go, but I wasn't very enthusiastic.

I felt quite daunted when we arrived as I had been taught this kind of preacher was wrong because he was neither homeless nor unmarried. I sat somewhat apprehensively since I really did not know what to expect, but it was unbelievable! I felt a sense of déjà vu.

The preacher, Dr Billy Graham, started talking about the wonder of God's saving grace, mercy and forgiveness in Jesus. Amazingly, the message was almost a repeat of the things Mervyn had told me. Jesus was the only person who could make us acceptable to God.

As I listened, the scales fell off my eyes! It was the strangest experience I have ever had. Suddenly everything was crystal clear. I saw exactly how wrong the 'true way' group message was. They believed and promoted their own efforts and way of doing things as the way to gain God's acceptance and approval. Other religions did the same thing.

Dr Graham then spoke about how religious activities or a belief that builds on works or legalism (rules and regulations) as a ticket to heaven is wrong. In fact it is actually cruel. It keeps people living on a knife-edge constantly wondering and worrying whether they will ever be good enough to be accepted by God when they die. The truth is that none of us will ever be good enough. The reality is:

Isaiah 64:6
We are all infected and impure with sin. When we display our righteous deeds, they are nothing but filthy rags.

We are not sinners because we sin; we sin because we are sinners! We have been born with a sin-nature that we inherited from Adam, our first human representative. No one is untouched by sin, and no one has the standard of perfection that God requires.

Hit like a Sledge-hammer!

I was a sinner!
 The penalty God had put on sin was death.
  God, in His grace and love, intervened.
   That penalty was paid by God Himself .
    He offered His own Son to cancel my debt of sin.
     Jesus died to obtain forgiveness for the
     debt of sin.
      Jesus rose from the dead to prove His
      payment was accepted by God!

Jesus had cleared my account!

I finally understood: only Jesus could make me acceptable to God,
only Jesus could give me eternal life.

Jesus was God's gift of grace to me received through faith and repentance.

A Time of Tears

Throughout that night I had no sleep. I wept. God, in His infinite grace and compassion, had answered my desperate prayer immeasurably. I was finally able to see what was missing in my life. Now it was my time to receive God's grace offered to me through Jesus. I prayed to my heavenly Father:

> *Thank you for your amazing grace.*
> *I know that I am a sinner and need forgiveness.*
> *I believe that Jesus died for my sins.*
> *I want to turn from my sins (repent).*
> *I now invite Jesus to come into my heart and life.*
> *Help me to trust and follow Jesus as long as I live.*
> *In Jesus' name,*
> *Amen.*

That night, I began a new, deeper relationship with Jesus. This revelation of grace was like the birth of a new life. The Holy Spirit was at work within, convicting and challenging me. I would never be the same again!

John 1:13

To all who believed Him and accepted Him, He gave the right to become children of God. They are reborn – not with a physical birth resulting from human passion or plan, but a birth that comes from God.

My heart broke for the 'true way' people. In anguish I lay prostrate on the floor. I found myself praying the same Biblical prayer as Esther:

Esther 8:3-6 (ESV)

How can I bear to see the calamity that is coming to my people? Or how can I bear to see the destruction of my kindred?

I saw the truth of the Scripture:

2 Corinthians 4:4

Satan, who is the god of this world, has blinded the minds of those who don't believe. They are unable to see the glorious light of the Good News.

The scales had fallen off my eyes. Now I had an awesome responsibility - I must tell others - but how was I going to do it? I knew the time had come when I had to make a stand. How was I going to explain the Good News of God's grace to a group that prided itself on the sacrifice or requirement of a homeless, unmarried preacher?

I was distraught. I was going to offend a great many people, including those I loved. How could I bear it?

Chapter Five

Cataclysmic Decision

Joshua 24:14-15 (ESV)

Choose this day whom you will serve. Put away the gods that your fathers served beyond the river and in Egypt and serve the Lord.

Breaking the News

Making a decision that pleases others is easy; however, making a decision that you know will displease, anger or upset others is another matter. It takes courage and resolve, strength and fortitude. Some decisions are insignificant, but others are very significant with far-reaching, irreversible consequences. We can find ourselves in situations when the decision we have to make will be cataclysmic. It will bring a time of great personal change, upheaval, distress and turmoil.

I desperately searched for an easier solution. I looked in vain for an alternative way. There was none, other than deciding to do nothing, but taking no action at all also had repercussions.

In Proverbs it warns of our responsibility to share with others what God has revealed to us:

Proverbs 24:11-13

Rescue those who are being unjustly sentenced to die; save them as they stagger to their death. Don't excuse yourself by saying 'Look, we didn't know.' For God understands all hearts and He sees you. He who guards your soul knows you knew. He will repay all people as their actions deserve.

This was my awesome responsibility. I was accountable to God, not people, no matter how much I loved them.

I thought of the far-reaching decisions Biblical women made in difficult situations. Esther made a courageous decision to risk her life for her captive people. As a consequence, a whole nation was saved. Ruth, a widow, made a selfless decision to care for her mother-in-law, Naomi, in a hostile, foreign land. The consequence of that decision led her on a path to a loving marriage. She became the great-grandparent of Israel's most famous King - King David - and a descendant in the lineage of Jesus Christ! All because she made the right decision at the right time!

However, other women made bad decisions. The most devastating cataclysmic decision in history was made by Eve. God had warned:

Genesis 2:16-17

You may freely eat the fruit of every tree in the garden – except the tree of knowledge of good and evil. If you eat its fruit, you are sure to die.

But Satan persuaded Eve to make a decision against God's authority. He contradicted God's warning and told a lie of epic proportions. He said:

Genesis 3:4

You won't die! God knows that your eyes will be opened as soon as you eat it and you will be like God, knowing both good and evil.

This statement appealed to her human pride. Eve ate the forbidden fruit and gave some to her husband, Adam. They thought eating the fruit would make them as wise as God.

The cold, chilling reality of that decision made them the very opposite! They became guilty sinners condemned to die.

Romans 5:12

When Adam sinned, sin entered the world. Adam's sin brought death, so death spread to everyone, for everyone sinned.

Yes, Eve received knowledge, but it was a knowledge she would rather not have received. She suddenly became aware of bad things. The knowledge of sin, lies, deceit, hate, death and destruction entered her mind. Too late she realized God had been protecting her. Her decision to disobey God's warning brought the devastating consequences of The Fall upon herself and all her descendants. The far-reaching, evil consequences were far beyond anything she could ever have dreamed of or thought about in her wildest imagination.

This story proved something vital to me. There are some decisions in life we cannot afford to get wrong; the consequences are too important. I thought about the relatively important decisions we make in this life: the person we decide to marry and share our life with; a career; the property we buy or the place we live. The most important decision we will ever make is whether or not to believe and follow Jesus. What can be more serious than a life or death decision?

God gave many warnings about Satan's character and craftiness. He said (of Satan):

John 8:44b

He was a murderer from the beginning. When he lies, he speaks out of his own character, for he is a liar and the father of lies.

I discerned that my fearful thoughts about the future were lying attacks from Satan. He was trying to prevent me from making a decision. He did not want me to move out of the 'true way' group. My fears were undermining my confidence in God's protection and provision over my life.

It was a matter of trust. Did I trust God enough to help me through whatever consequences I might have to face? Did I truly believe God could provide all I might need in the future? Could I trust God to strengthen me to cope with opposition or even being abandoned or ostracized?

My father could be so angry when opposed. As for my mother, her health was not good. What if my decision had an even further detrimental effect? I knew that if I let these factors deter me I would never make it. I had to trust God to take care of all these things.

There are moments in life that are indescribable. This was definitely one of them. The pressure I felt was so intense that I felt nauseous. Telling my parents was the hardest thing I have ever done. Neither of them could understand my decision at all. They were devastated and furiously angry. They refused either to listen to any explanation or believe that I had hidden my unhappiness for years. As far as they were concerned, I had been deceived. I was leaving the only 'true way' on the earth. I was making a decision I would regret for the rest of my life. Worse still, I was on my way to hell.

I tried to explain the difference between human religious achievements and the gift of grace through Jesus. It was like showing a red rag to a bull. My father almost charged at me, so great was his rage. My decision was certainly having a cataclysmic effect. I was distraught at causing so much distress to those I loved. It got worse. My father blamed

Mervyn: if I had never met him I would still be 'happy' in the 'true way' group!

As the news filtered around the 'true way' group, a few members kindly telephoned to express concern. Apart from that, there was little communication. I was too upset after the experience with my parents to talk to anyone. I didn't even feel able to answer the telephone. I leaned heavily on Mervyn during this transitional time, but he was concerned that I was hiding away from people as if I had done something very wrong. I don't know why I felt like this. I just couldn't deal with any more anger or hostility. I suppose I wanted to avoid further distressing confrontations.

I wondered what would have happened if I had done this without Mervyn's support. The very reaction I had to deal with now was the reason I had felt too scared to discuss my feelings sooner. If they didn't believe me now, would they have believed me earlier? I doubted it very much.

I Will Never Leave You

It was strange adjusting to life outside the walls of the 'true way' group. I had not known anything else since I had been born. At times it was quite overwhelming. I struggled to cope with the separation from my old lifestyle. In some ways it felt like a huge bereavement, as though I had lost everything I had known since childhood all at once, but despite all the outward turmoil I had an inner peace. It didn't matter what might happen to me in the future. I was now ready to meet with God.

Sometimes I would still struggle with periods of fear. It was particularly hard when Mervyn had to go away on a long business trip. I was taken aback at how anxious I became. The downside of having a good imagination is that I started to think of all the things that could go wrong. I wondered what I should do if I had an accident like chopping off my hand in the kitchen!

In this state of mind I waved Mervyn off. I was trying to stem the tide of inner panic. Tears were not far away, but then something wonderful happened. I heard a special voice speaking behind me. It was gentle yet powerful. I spun around in shock. I knew it was the voice of Jesus. How thrilling! He was speaking directly to me! An awesome presence surrounded me as He spoke the sweetest words that are engraved on my heart:

Hebrews13:5 (ESV)
I will never leave you or forsake you.

It was His promise to me, and I know He will always keep it. He will always be close by in my life and death.

I felt that Jesus wanted me to really trust Him. When I was on my own, it was a test of how much trust I had in Him to take care of me. No matter how isolated and alone I was from the life I had known, Jesus was all I needed. He was bigger than any problem or calamity that might befall me.

However, fear soon raised its ugly head again. My father came to the house shouting with intimidating threats. He wished he had a shot-gun so he could shoot us! I was distraught and deeply ashamed of my father's behaviour. I worried about what harm he might do to Mervyn. He seemed particularly furious with him.

But it didn't seem to faze Mervyn. He simply said that if he did get killed, he'd be better off. He would exchange this place for his home in heaven with Jesus - the safest and happiest place anyone could be!

I realised that where there is a strong trust in God, there is also a powerful peace. The fruit of faith or trust is peace. No matter how wildly the storm beats around that person, it cannot take away a peace that is supernaturally given. The heart that trusts has peace. It doesn't look at the storm; it looks at the person above the storm: Jesus.

I thought of the advice that the Apostle Paul gave:

Philippians 4:6-7
Don't worry about anything; instead, pray about everything. Tell God what you need, and thank Him for all He has done. Then you will experience God's peace, which exceeds anything we can understand. His peace will guard your hearts and minds as you live in Christ Jesus.

There was a promise in this verse that I had never seen before. I had to make it real in my life if I wanted to experience supernatural peace. My part was to take my worries and fears to God in prayer but with a thankful attitude for what He had already done in my life. Then God would fulfil His part by filling me with His supernatural peace.

Rehabilitation Time

There were many times when I felt like a square peg in a round hole. I wondered how many people have prayed asking to be made normal. I just wanted to be normal! I loved the Biblical story of the potter working in the potter's house, which illustrated God's rehabilitating and restorative work.

Jeremiah 18:3b-4

...and the potter was working at his wheel. But the jar he was making did not turn out as he had hoped, so he crushed it into a lump of clay again and started over.

With my life now fully in God's hands it could be started over again. He could make me into something completely different. I would become a new creation. I could be remade into what He wanted me to be. I would then be a vessel whose transformation would glorify God's gracious power working in my life.

The first major personal change I made was my hair. I wanted to get rid of the bun style; it would save me so much time. It wasn't easy to have my hair cut shorter, and I wondered if something awful would happen to me if I went against this teaching. I thought of the story of Samson and Delilah. When this wicked woman cut off his hair he became weak and unable to defend himself against his enemies (Judges 16).

I knew that what I was doing was completely different. But I was still absolutely terrified. It was such an ordeal when the hairdresser started to snip away. I just sat with my eyes closed and prayed as perspiration ran down my forehead. The hairdresser remarked that I looked very pale and shivery. She wondered if I was coming down with something! How could I tell her that I was wondering if I would die if I had my hair shortened! It would sound absolutely ridiculous. Happily, I discovered I didn't fall down and die.

It certainly made me look different, but more importantly it made me feel different. I had gotten rid of a weight on top of both my head and my mind! This experience gave me confidence and so I made other decisions about my appearance and dress code. I began to dress in the way I felt comfortable and which reflected my own personality.

A pattern began to emerge. Whenever I went to change or do anything different from what I had been taught, I struggled with guilt and fear, as if something awful might happen. This constant battle was draining. I started to question my reactions. Why did I feel guilty? Where did it say in the Bible that I shouldn't do this? Why was I afraid of doing a particular thing? Did that fear come from others? Was it something I had done in the past to please people or God?

This was a fascinating process. It helped me so much in making decisions I had never been allowed to make before. I began to overcome my guilt and fear reactions.

2 Timothy 1:7
For God has not given us a spirit of fear and timidity, but of power, love and self-discipline.

Mervyn dedicated a verse of Scripture to me. I was to make this my aim in my daily life, particularly through difficult and perplexing times.

Proverbs 3:5-6 (ESV)
Trust in the Lord with all your heart; lean not on your own understanding. Acknowledge Him in all your ways and He will direct your paths.

In difficult times, we question why certain things happen. We cannot find any sense or reason in a tragedy or our difficult circumstances. Worse still, we may even question if God has left us or is punishing us for a bad decision we have made; yet whatever our feelings, Jesus said:

John 6:37
Whoever comes to me I will never turn away.

In times such as these, we need to ignore our changing emotions. We have to cling to Jesus whose love is unchanging. We need to remember that Satan comes to taunt and torment us when we are at our most vulnerable. But this is the time when the reality of our faith is tested. Is our faith limited to the good times, or can it endure hardship and bad times? Will we stand firm and keep our trust anchored in Jesus to guide us through those dark times, or will we turn away in bitterness and anger? Again, it is a decision that we have to make when bad things happen to us personally. Through each difficult experience I have sought to follow my dedicated verse which has become so special to me over the years.

Being set free from our past may happen quickly, or it may be a step-by-step process. It took years to overcome the mind-controlling doctrine instilled into me as a child. I have met people who are struggling with drug or alcohol withdrawal symptoms. As they fight to overcome the difficult and extremely distressing symptoms, I can empathize in a way they find remarkable. There is a parallel similarity when withdrawing from a legalistic religion. Its withdrawal symptoms can be brutal and distressing too. I hadn't bargained for the enormous reactions I would have when I moved into territory that had been forbidden in the past.

Breaking the Spirit Of Fear

I knew Jesus was with me. He had confirmed it to me in a very personal way, but I still struggled with fear and anxiety. I thought of the many times Jesus said to His disciples, "Fear not!" or "Don't be afraid! I am here!" or "Where is your faith?" Jesus had to say the same things to me innumerable times, and He still does!

I wanted to overcome my fear of people, their disapproval and criticism, intimidation and threats. Jesus warned:

Luke 12:4-5

Dear friends, don't be afraid of those who want to kill your body, they cannot do any more to you after that. But I'll tell you whom to fear. Fear God, who has the power to kill you and then throw you into hell. Yes, He's the one to fear.

I should be more concerned with God's reaction to the things I did and said, not the reactions of others around me.

A psalm also helped me to deal with my fears:

Psalms 56:4

But when I am afraid,
I will put my trust in you.
I praise God for what He has promised.
I trust in God, so why should I be afraid?
What can mere mortals do to me?

This was the pattern I followed. Whenever I was afraid, I took my fears to Jesus. I trusted Him to deal with the situation. I could expect two things: He would either make the situation change or He would show me how I was to change things myself. If it were the latter then I also was to trust Him to give me the power to take action and confront those fears.

Mervyn wrote a song for me called 'Out of Egypt'. Although it was a re-play of the exodus of the children of Israel from Egypt, he saw it all as a parallel to my exit from the 'true way' group. I was Moses and he was Aaron. Egypt was the bondage of my hard religion. Pharaoh represented the people I had to tell of my decision. Through my fear I was to focus on the promise of God that He would certainly be with me (Exodus 3-5).

OUT OF EGYPT

Verse 1:

Many years ago while slaves in Egypt,
God looked down in pity on His own,
Struggling day by day beneath their burdens,
Knowing how they longed to be back home.

Chorus:

Certainly I will be with you,
There's no need to fear or dread
I will bring my people out of Egypt,
Tell the Pharaoh what I Am hath said.

Verse 2:

God chose Moses for this special mission,
A humble man, unsure if he should go.
Trembling at the thought of meeting Pharaoh,
How to find the words he didn't know.

Verse 3:

For a while the Pharaoh's heart was hardened,
He still refused to listen or obey.
But when God sent His mighty plagues on Egypt,
Pharaoh sent God's people on their way.

Verse 4:

And so today we won't be slaves in Egypt,
Through Christ Jesus our escape's been made.
We shall be set free from modern Egypt,
If we just remember what I Am hath said.

Chorus:

Certainly I will be with you,
There's no need to fear or dread.
See, I've brought my people out of Egypt,
Remember what the Great I Am hath said!

This song has been an inspiration to me whenever I feel alone and afraid.

Church Phobia

The greatest challenge of all was to attend a church service. Fear paralyzed me at the thought of going into a church, never mind sitting through a whole service! A phobia is an exaggerated fear. People have phobias of all kinds of things, be it spiders, snakes or flying. Without realizing it, I had developed a phobia of attending religious meetings. I would do anything to avoid putting myself in a situation where I might encounter an atmosphere I had experienced in the 'true way' group meetings. I found attending Christian meetings a huge ordeal; I worried in case I would encounter that awful evil-like presence, and I would start to tremble and perspire hours before we left the house. It took years to integrate into church life.

At times I thought that I would never overcome my reactions. I hate fear. I hate anxiety. Unless they are overcome they will ruin your life and prevent you from helping others. But the antidote to fear and anxiety is faith and trust in Jesus. As I exercised trust in Jesus to help me through each experience, I noticed how little by little my reactions diminished. Sometimes I would fail miserably, but I was encouraged to read that some of the disciples had struggled with their fears and failures. Yet Jesus had still used them to work mightily for Him by spreading the Good News of the Gospel of grace. There was still hope for me!

I questioned why God didn't just give me immediate release from the difficulties I encountered. He gave me this answer:

Exodus 23:30 (ESV)
Little by little I will drive them out from before you, until you have increased and possess the land.

It was through a gradual process that I was to be taught valuable lessons about life. There were things God wanted me to learn. I could not learn these important lessons through a quick and easy release. God knows exactly what He is doing, even if the process seems long and drawn out. Through every nook and cranny of our lives He wants to develop our character into the image of His Son, Jesus.

Reading the Bible without Blinkers

I was challenged to read the Bible from the beginning to the end, but I was to read it as though it was for the very first time. I had to wipe from my mind all the preconceived ideas and things I had already been taught. This was a most amazing experience. I was stunned at how much I saw that I hadn't seen before, yet it was still the same Bible. This challenge made me realize the importance of always praying for the Holy Spirit to give a revelation of God's word. It was through this method that so many misconceptions I had were cleared away.

A Kitchen Experience

There were times when deep sorrow for the people I had known overwhelmed me. I longed to be able to share with them God's amazing grace. One day in the kitchen, I took my sadness and pain to Jesus. As I cried to him, I was lifted in my spirit to another dimension. That is the only way I can describe it. I had already had an experience of the Holy Spirit gently touching my tongue. It had been so light, just like a dove landing very gently. I had been given a new heavenly language. It enabled me to express my deepest emotions to God in a different way. It was such a beautiful, gentle and reverent experience.

I was moved to speak in my new heavenly language. I was filled with the most intense and profound joy, the like of which I had never experienced before. The message given was based on the following words of Scripture:

Nehemiah 8:10b
The joy of the Lord is your strength.

John 16:22b
No one will take your joy from you.

Ever since that moment my joy has remained - the joy of the Good News of grace found through faith in Jesus and the joy of His personal presence in my life. This has helped me to come through some lonely and perplexing situations.

Reconciliation

I constantly prayed for my parents. Approximately eighteen months after I had left the 'true way' I was convicted to seek reconciliation. I believed I would have no peace within me until I had done so.

My knees knocked as I rang the doorbell of my parents' home. I dreaded my father answering the door, but he appeared to be really pleased to see me, as did my mother. On that day we were reconciled. I now had another day I would always remember. I was so glad that I had obeyed that call on my heart. I thanked God for his love and mercy in reconciling me with my parents. He had softened their hearts to accept me. However, whenever I tried to talk about my decision to leave the 'true way' group the barriers immediately came up, so I prayed for patience and wisdom.

I love the following passage:

Psalm 37:4-7

Take delight in the Lord,
And He will give you your heart's desires.
Commit everything you do to the Lord.
Trust Him and He will help you.
He will make your innocence radiate like the dawn
And the justice of your cause will shine like the noonday sun.
Be still in the presence of the Lord
And wait patiently for Him to act.

I could patiently wait for God to move. He would open doors of opportunity to share the peace and grace that I had found in Jesus.

At last, everything seemed to be falling into place. My heart was filled with tremendous hope for the future. Now, nothing could go wrong - or could it?

Chapter Six

Hit by a Tornado

Romans 8:28 (ESV)
*And we know, for those who love God, all things work
for good for those who are called according to His purpose.*

Devastating News

Mervyn started to become tired and listless. Since this was so unusual it made me feel a little bit uneasy. He then developed an irritating dry cough and got a prescription for antibiotics, but the cough still persisted. When he saw the doctor again he was diagnosed with hay fever and given an inhaler to relieve the cough, yet after a few months of trying this there was no improvement. His doctor insisted that he should persist with the inhaler, however.

Mervyn decided to see the Occupational Health Doctor at his work for a second opinion. Again, he was told there was nothing wrong, but a few months later he developed spasmodic pain in his right leg and lower spine. The doctor thought it was sciatica, and strong painkillers and rest were prescribed. But the pain steadily progressed so that he could hardly walk despite having his medication increased. My uneasiness cascaded into full-blown anxiety. It was obvious to me that things were getting worse, not better. I also worried if Mervyn was anaemic, due to his pallor and exhaustion. I persuaded him to ask for a blood test.

This started a roller-coaster of events that shocked us deeply. The results of the test were serious; Mervyn was dangerously anaemic and could have a heart attack at any time! I felt as though I had been hit by a tornado. I knew then that something was seriously wrong.

An emergency blood transfusion was arranged. A transfusion is a strange, almost unearthly experience to watch. But it is also awesome. Someone else's blood can transfer life to another person immediately. Life was in that blood. It reminded me of what God said in Leviticus:

Leviticus 17:11a
...for the life of the body is in its blood.

I saw how true that was, and I wondered about the persons who had freely given blood. I found I could not begin to describe my emotion or gratitude towards them.

Although overcome with gratitude, I was also overcome with anger. Why had it taken so long for this to be noticed? My head buzzed with questions and lots of "if only's". *If only* I had insisted this test be done much sooner. *If only* I had insisted a visit to someone else for a health check. *If only* I had challenged the diagnosis. I was back to my "if only's" again. It is a complete waste of time and energy. "If only's" cannot change anything in the past. I had to focus on the present. I prayed that a speedy diagnosis of the problem could be found and successfully treated.

Over the next month there were non-stop investigations and tests. There was also non-stop worry and non-stop prayer. By now Mervyn was unable to walk at all as the pain was too excruciating, but despite the pain medication being doubled he could not get any relief, day or night.

I started pushing him around in a wheelchair. He hated it and so did I. I would disappear to wipe away my hidden tears at his pain, his indignity, his increasing helplessness. I constantly prayed to God to take away the pain, but it became steadily worse.

Tsunami Time

The date arrived for the results of the scan. It is another day that is etched on my mind and stands out above other days. My insides were in a knot as I entered the consultant's room. I was instantly aware of the strained atmosphere, but it was the compassion in the nurse's eyes that hit me. It told me to prepare for the worst. I realized I was in a bad and good news room - a room where the "you're going to live" or "you're going to die" announcements take place. It's horrid. It tears you apart.

I remember thinking we weren't created for this. God did not create us to die; He created us to live. That is why we find these situations unbearable. I braced myself as those awful words were spoken.

"I'm sorry. I'm afraid it's not good news."

One kidney had a tumour. They believed it was cancer, and it may have spread to the spinal cord.

As soon as I heard the word 'cancer', my heart shattered. It's a word that everyone dreads. I shuddered from head to toe. I felt as though a knife had been plunged into my heart. Now I know what it's like to be overwhelmed by a tsunami. A massive wave of pain and anguish engulfed me, sweeping away my hopes and joy for the future.

World's Best Preacher Returns

I was staring into the face of the world's best preacher once again - the preacher with the horrible name Death. Was he going to haunt me with the possibility of another sermon? Disbelief rose up inside me. I also felt fear. It seemed to grab hold of my throat and grip it tightly. I felt as though I could no longer breathe. Why was this happening to us? Why?

Then my faith kicked in. Maybe God was allowing this to happen so His power of healing could be displayed. A healing would be an awesome witness. How many people would be impressed if that were to happen? I believed God could do such a thing if He wanted, but what if God didn't want to heal Mervyn? What if God wanted to take Mervyn home to be with Him in heaven? What then? What would my reaction be if God allowed my personal hopes and dreams to be smashed into pieces? What would happen to my faith in a good God then?

I am not sure how I managed to drive home safely that day. I did everything on autopilot. It was as though someone else was dealing with the necessary process. I was away on a completely different planet. I was numb with shock.

An appointment with a surgeon had been arranged to discuss surgery. The cancer was the type that did not respond to chemotherapy. It was too aggressive. If the cancer had spread to other organs the prognosis was poor. It was hard taking all this information in. My brain was whizzing around, trying to absorb it all and the consequences of perhaps there being no curative treatment. It meant that Death, the world's best preacher, would be delivering a very powerful and personally devastating sermon.

All Things?

Mervyn was calm as he sipped his cup of tea at the kitchen table. I was the complete opposite though; I frantically paced up and down as I was too distraught to sit still. I had faced bad moments before, but they were nothing compared to this. Nothing had prepared me for this awful, scared feeling. This was by far the worst moment in my life. I contemplated my future that had suddenly and drastically changed.

I knew Mervyn was not afraid of dying. He completely believed the Scripture:

2 Corinthians 5:6-8
So we are always confident, even though we know that as long as we live in these bodies we are not at home with the Lord. For we live by believing and not by seeing. Yes, we are fully confident that we would rather be away from these earthly bodies, for then we will be at home with the Lord.

Mervyn actually looked forward to that moment when he would exchange this life for a heavenly one.

He tried to reassure me. He did not want me to be afraid or distressed. He believed that if this was his time to go, I would be given strength; God would be there to help me. But I was afraid. Deep down, in a selfish place, I was afraid of what my world would be like without him in it. Like angry wasps stinging me viciously, the questions circled round and round. Would I cope? Would my faith hold? What about my finances? What about the future? It seemed like everything I had built was now suddenly crashing down around me. The feelings that overwhelmed me were unlike anything in my previous experience.

But the next moment is forever etched on my mind. I remember how Mervyn sat at the kitchen table with an expression of peace and quiet resignation on his face as he spoke. He said, "Remember what it says: 'All things work for good.'" I realised that he was quoting from a Bible verse he loved:

Romans 8:28 (ESV)
And we know that for those who love God all things work together for good, for those who are called according to His purpose.

Stunned by this attitude, I stared in disbelief.

"All things?" I questioned incredulously. "How can all things work for good? What's good about cancer?"

Of course, I knew that there was nothing good about it. Cancer was evil. It was the promise in the verse Mervyn wanted me to cling to. He wanted me to trust God, despite my anguish. He believed that God would then use our faith to work through this experience for the good and wellbeing of others.

In tears, I listened intently as Mervyn said, "I am ready to go and be with Jesus. You know there is no better place anyone could be. We all have to go at some point, some of us sooner than others. God works in ways that you and I can't see or understand.

"In eternity we will understand why He allowed this to happen, but for now He wants to see if we can trust Him. It's in the darkest times that our faith shines the brightest."

We talk about 'awesome moments'. This was definitely one. Mervyn's faith comforted and strengthened me. I felt ashamed. I thought it was ironic that the verse started with "And we know". In fact, I *didn't* know and trust God the way Mervyn did, but I wanted to. I looked into his peaceful face and I was overwhelmed. His response to such a devastating diagnosis was simply to trust God. He wasn't agitated about it like I was.

I had much to learn about clinging to God's promises through bad times. I thought of the special Bible verse Mervyn had given me:

Proverbs 3:5a
Trust in the Lord with all your heart, do not depend on your own understanding...

I had to trust God when I could not understand why. If I didn't, Satan would use this experience to make me believe that God did not care - or worse still, that God had abandoned us.

I began to pray that the promise in Romans 8:28 would become a personal reality - that God would work through my pain and sorrow to bring something good out of it. I could then share this verse in an inspirational way to help and comfort others.

The Apostle Paul understood this concept. He wrote:

2 Corinthians 1:4
[God] comforts us in all our troubles so that we can comfort others. When they are troubled, we will be able to give them the same comfort God has given us.

Romans 8:28 Rainbow

Into my mind came the picture of a rainbow. It had been created by God as a sign of His promise to Noah and his descendants. God promised that He would never flood the earth in the same way again. He said:

Genesis 9:13

I have placed my rainbow in the clouds. It is a sign of my covenant with you and with all the earth.

God had brought cataclysmic judgment through the rainstorm. Now the rainbow, a meteorological phenomenon associated with the rainstorm, would be a perfect image of peace for all the earth. In the midst of a fierce storm the appearance of a rainbow would bring reassurance and comfort. What a beautiful reminder of God's promise.

Suddenly, with a flash of insight, I saw how Romans 8:28 shone like a rainbow of promises above the devastating storms in my life. This was amazing! God was creating something special for me out of this verse, but there was a condition: I had to trust Him despite my pain. Only then could He use me to display this rainbow of comfort to benefit others around me.

In my mind God created a combination of seven promises. These were to be displayed over the rainstorms in my life. They reminded me of the seven perfectly combined colours found in a rainbow:-

A promise of comfort
A promise of hope
A promise of reassurance
A promise of peace
A promise of purpose
A promise of blessing
A promise of joy

I had comfort because God would work all things for my eternal good.

I had hope because with God no situation is hopeless.

I had reassurance because God would certainly[3] go with me. I was not alone!

I had peace because God was in control.

I had purpose because God had a plan for me.

I had blessing because God had chosen me.

I had joy because God loved me.

This was my Romans 8:28 rainbow of seven promises. It helped me to make a decision. I would trust God when nothing made sense. Through the storms and tears, through the trauma and anguish, I would hold on to this rainbow of promises. Maybe one day I would see how God did indeed work to produce something good out of my pain.

Faith believes there is a purpose in every tragedy He allows. We cannot see it - we have an earth-bound perspective - but God works from the perspective of eternity. That is why we have to exercise faith and trust in Him. When we trust Him through the bad times, He will work to use it to build our character for His eternal plan and purpose.

It is so easy to say things about your faith to impress others when everything is going well, but when we go through troubles or tragic circumstances, the reality of what we believe - of who we really trust - shines through. It is in those moments that our faith is exposed as deep or shallow, real or fake. I looked into Mervyn's face. I saw clearly a faith and love that shone brightly despite the awful verdict. It was awesome.

From Bad to Worse

My faith was to be tested further. Have you ever prayed for things to get better and instead they got worse? Nothing prepared me for this situation. Nor did it prepare me for the pain of the days and months that followed. It is so difficult to watch someone you love gradually deteriorate.

---

[3] From 'Out of Egypt' song (see page 64)

Yet throughout this time I was privileged to see a faith which grew stronger, despite the increasing pain and immobility.

The Apostle Paul wrote:

2 Corinthians 4:16

That is why we never give up. Though our bodies are dying, our spirits are being renewed every day.

I saw the reality of this in Mervyn's life.

Mervyn's condition worsened. The doctor increased his medication again, but he could still hardly move. On the day of his consultant's appointment a terrible spasm gripped his spine making any kind of movement agony. Mervyn decided I should attend the consultation on his behalf and explain the problem. I found this a difficult thing to do as I was unsure what the reaction would be when I wasn't the patient, but we were in a desperate situation.

As I drove to the hospital I found myself praying the opening verses from Psalm 61:

Psalm 61:1-2a

O God, listen to my cry! Hear my prayer! From the ends of the earth, I cry to you for help when my heart is overwhelmed.

God heard and strengthened me. I simply could not have done it in my own strength.

In the waiting room, I met a kind stranger. I knew that God had arranged this because it was so extraordinary. This lady appeared to sense my inward distress. As soon as she understood my predicament she disappeared. It seemed she had gone off to get help for me and Mervyn! She brought a lovely nurse who took care of me and offered me a drink of tea. Apparently, I looked so white and shaky that they thought I was going to collapse!

The consultant was a very caring and empathetic lady - not at all what I expected. It had been so distressing to leave Mervyn alone at home, but it worked for our good. He was admitted that morning as an emergency and radiotherapy treatment immediately started. The scan had revealed secondary tumours around the spinal cord. These were pressing on the nerves causing excruciating pain and immobility, but the primary tumour was in the kidney. The plan of action was to treat the secondary spinal tumours first and then operate to remove the kidney. Obviously sciatica had been a completely wrong diagnosis. The situation was far more serious than either of us had been led to believe.

We were then to have another devastating blow. After further tests, cancer deposits were found in Mervyn's lungs. There was a serious reason for his constant cough after all. We were told that a brain scan was essential. There could be no surgery if cancer deposits had moved to the brain. We were both completely overwhelmed by this possibility.

There are times when you have to cling tightly to the hand of Jesus. This was one of them. I cried all night, pleading for this scan to be clear. Through the long, dark hours until the early morning light appeared, I prayed. I was exhausted, stiff and cold. What a night! However, I discovered a life-changing lesson. God is bigger than any blow we receive. In His time He can cut through our anguish with His peace.

How I hate cancer! It is a wicked, evil disease. It has a kind of mental torture too; no-one knows where it's going to strike next. But this time we had good news. The brain scan was clear. I was ecstatic! Now things could move ahead. The operation was scheduled and more radiotherapy planned. Hope started to rise for the future. Things seemed to be heading in the right direction at last.

Prayers for Healing

I prayed constantly for Mervyn's healing. If it wasn't going to be a miraculous healing, it would be through the medical staff. I kept a journal. I wrote a record of my prayers and the eventual answers. I saw how God helped me to deal with each situation that was thrown at me. God's presence and warmth steadied me. At times I felt like a lost child who didn't know the way. I could only cling to the hand that held mine as it guided me along a dark and treacherous path.

The prayers of faithful friends, the church and relatives at this time meant so much. I cannot express my gratitude adequately for all the prayers on Mervyn's behalf and mine.

I started to study the various healings that took place in the Bible. I loved the story of King Hezekiah (2 Kings 20). He had been diagnosed with an incurable disease also. God advised him to put his affairs in order before he died. But when Hezekiah wept and pleaded with God to intervene and heal him, he was granted a further fifteen years to live.

I found this fascinating. I compared our situation to King Hezekiah's. God knew all about our situation too. Was this Mervyn's time to die? We had made a will. All our affairs were in order. I wondered if God would intervene in answer to all the prayers on Mervyn's behalf. Maybe God would let him live another fifteen years too?

But I noticed the down side about extending Hezekiah's life. In his further lifespan he greatly displeased God. I would want to die when I was pleasing God. That would be Mervyn's choice too. It was food for thought. Mervyn believed we should pray for God's will to be done. We knew God had healed others, but we also knew those whom God hadn't healed. Some things are simply a mystery.

Mervyn loved the attitude of three friends of an Old Testament Prophet called Daniel. These men were called Shadrach, Meshach, and Abednego (Daniel 3). They refused to obey an order to bow down and worship the king's statue. The punishment for their defiance was death in a fiery furnace.

They responded by saying:

Daniel 3:17-18

If we are thrown into the blazing furnace, the God whom we serve is able to save us. He will rescue us from your power, Your Majesty. But even if He doesn't, we want to make it clear to you, Your Majesty, that we will never serve your gods or worship the gold statue you have set up.

They believed that God could work a miracle on their behalf. But if God decided not to intervene and save them, it made no difference to their decision. They trusted God with the result.

The question was: could I trust God with the right result for Mervyn's life? Mervyn knew I was wrestling in prayer for him to be healed. He believed that God had a plan and purpose for his life. It was planned even before he was born. When that plan was complete he would be called home in whatever way God's sovereign will permitted. It could be through a heart attack, a car accident, a plane crash or a disease like cancer.

The Psalmist understood this important fact when he wrote:

Psalm 139:16

You saw me before I was born. Every day of my life was recorded in your book. Every moment was laid out before a single day had passed.

Mervyn trusted God with his future.

Psalm 31:15

My future is in your hands.

Only God knew the future for both of us.

Would my Romans 8:28 rainbow of comforting promises shine brightly through the perilous days ahead? Would they be enough to help me live under the storm clouds of doubt and fear as I faced an uncertain future? Only time would show.

Chapter Seven

Everything Falls Apart

1 Corinthians 10:13b

God is faithful. He will not allow the temptation to be more than you can stand.

A House Move

The operation to remove the kidney was successful. The consultant gave Mervyn a prognosis of twelve to eighteen months although he could have more time; it all depended on the level of cancer cell activity, but this was difficult to predict.

We talked about the future. Mervyn was keen to return to his office, even if it was for a couple of hours each day. He was now able to shuffle around with the aid of two walking sticks, but a wheelchair was needed for long distances. The problem was driving the long journey. It was a round trip of more than fifty miles a day to work. We had tried to move nearer his work in the past without success. I suggested we would consider trying to move house again. If we moved closer, I could easily drive Mervyn to his workplace.

We prayed about it. We decided if God wanted us to move it would happen quickly. It did. Within twenty four hours of calling an estate agent, the house was sold and a contract arranged to move in exactly six weeks time! It was exhausting visiting the hospital and dealing with the house sale at the same time. I had never moved house before. I had no idea of the endless paperwork and preparation needed. But by the time Mervyn was discharged from hospital everything was organised. He was amazed at all I had managed to achieve - and so was I!

Both of us were looking forward to a new start in a new place. My constant prayer was that Mervyn would live beyond the timescale given by the consultant. I began to feel really hopeful that my prayer would be answered.

Everything Falls Apart

After a week at home, Mervyn suddenly developed severe back pain. His back had locked in a lopsided kind of sitting position. Another scan was urgently organised, but it was impossible for him to lie flat to go through it. Two doctors were called to administer morphine injections. They made no difference. I was crying helplessly as I listened to his harrowing screams of agony. Eventually they compromised with a standard x-ray machine.

The earth-shattering verdict hit me like a destructive earthquake. Mervyn would never walk again, nor would he be able to lie in a flat position again. Both of us were devastated. I could not hide my anguish and distress. The x-rays showed that the strong radiotherapy had made his lower vertebrae disintegrate. There was enormous pressure on the spinal cord. Now every jolt or movement made him shudder in agony and break out in a sweat.

It seemed to me that Mervyn was being tested like Job. Job was a man who lived in Old Testament days; he relentlessly experienced one disaster after another. Job was a righteous man whom God allowed Satan to test, yet after losing his home, his business, his children and finally his health, Job could still say:

Job 13:15 (AKJ)
Though [God] slay me, yet will I trust Him.

Job's wife reacted differently. She challenged Job to turn against God. She said:

Job 2:9
Are you still trying to maintain your integrity? Curse God and die.

This was the exact reaction that Satan wanted to provoke from Job, but despite his agony Job remained firm. He replied:

Job 2:10
"You talk like a foolish woman. Should we accept only good things from the hand of God and never anything bad?" So in all this, Job said nothing wrong.

Job's steadfast faith in such dire circumstances inspired me so much; I did not want to end up like Job's wife.

Mervyn's pain was excruciating. At times it almost drove him over the edge. He never slept properly. Sometimes when he did sleep his spine would go into a spasm. This would cause him intense agony. It was a never-ending task to keep pulling him back into a position that would give him the most relief. We both prayed for healing, constantly. Sometimes I would lay my hands on him and plead with God to heal him instantly. I was very persistent. I was determined never to give up praying for this.

Mervyn insisted we go through all his documentation. He wanted to make sure I would be able to sort things out if necessary. I didn't like doing this; it seemed to underscore the fragile nature of our situation and make it a reality. I realised that subconsciously I hadn't accepted that Mervyn had a terminal disease. I had also refused to consider that he may not be healed. Denial can be a self-coping mechanism, but unfortunately it just puts off dealing with reality.

Going Through Fire and Flood

Four days before we were due to move, everything fell apart again. Mervyn had been extremely unwell all day. At 2:00am he began to hallucinate. He became disorientated, so I called the Emergency Doctor. I looked outside anxiously; it was snowing hard. A strong wind was beating against the house. It was not a good night for anyone to be travelling. I was scared. Was Mervyn going to die? I had never seen anyone become so suddenly ill before.

The doctor arranged emergency hospital admittance. He tried to prepare me for the worst. I was desperately trying to keep calm. Inside I was a shivering wreck. The next part was just too horrid and too awful for words. It took the two ambulance men exactly thirty minutes to get Mervyn inside the ambulance. It seemed like hours. He was so difficult to move. He was hallucinating and thrashing around. I shook with relief when they eventually got him inside. They hurtled off with all the lights flashing. I hurriedly locked up the house and followed in my car.

The twenty minute journey to the hospital was a nightmare. The visibility on the motorway was poor due to the snow. I was driving as fast as I could under the circumstances; I was desperate to catch up with the ambulance. The roads were slippery and dangerous as they were frozen with ice.

I thought I would never reach the hospital. I could not see anything ahead. I could only peer through my windscreen at the swirling snow. I desperately prayed for God to help me arrive safely and to keep Mervyn safe until I arrived. I was berating myself for not travelling with him in the ambulance. I should not have left him alone. I wanted to be with him if he was going to die. I was in a state of full-blown panic as I dashed up the long, seemingly never-ending corridors. Hospitals are eerie places at night; every room seemed deserted and quiet.

The next forty eight hours were horrendous. The doctor warned me that Mervyn's condition was serious. Levels of calcium in his blood were abnormally high indicating a high level of cancer activity. He also had a severe water infection. This would be treated with intravenous drugs, but there was nothing they could do to stop the cancer now attacking his body.

I asked the doctor to start a saline drip. I knew Mervyn was dehydrated, but almost an hour passed without any action. His condition was deteriorating. I tried again and again to get someone to put a drip in his arm.

Mervyn was disorientated. He kept resisting anyone who tried to hold his arm. The nurse refused to do it so I desperately tried - but he wouldn't keep still. Time after time I tried to get water down his throat, but he couldn't seem to be able to swallow. There seemed to be so few staff on duty to attend to patients; there were even patients waiting on stretchers in the ward corridor for attention. It was a hopeless and utterly chaotic situation.

I Can't Take Any More

I cannot tell you how many times I cried out to God, "I can't take it anymore. It's just too hard to bear."

I pleaded with Jesus. "Don't let his life end this way – please help me find someone to put a drip in his arm." I was almost beside myself at this point. I felt as though I was in an impossible situation. God had abandoned us.

Psalm 69 came to mind.

Psalm 69:1-3

Save me, O God for the floodwaters are up to my neck. Deeper and deeper I sink into the mire; I can't find a foothold, I am in deep water and the floods overwhelm me. I am exhausted from crying for help; my throat is parched. My eyes are swollen with weeping, waiting for my God to help me.

Suddenly my Romans 8:28 rainbow appeared. It steadied me. I remembered God's promises.

1 Corinthians 10:13b
And God is faithful. He will not allow the temptation to be more than you can stand. When you are tempted, He will show you a way out so that you can endure.

I cried out to God again. "Please don't let him die this way - not here; I just couldn't bear it."

Eventually a nurse helped me, and Mervyn calmed down. He let me hold his arm as a drip was put in. He had been admitted at 4:00am. I had persevered for over ten hours to get a drip organized.

I began to discern a difference in his appearance. He became normal and lucid. Jesus had been merciful. I know that He preserved Mervyn's life. There could be no other explanation. My prayer had been answered. Jesus had delayed Mervyn's move to heaven in answer to my heart's cry: "Not yet, not now, not this way - please, Jesus."

Wearily I left the hospital and returned home. After all, I still had to move house in just two days' time. It seemed crazy now under the circumstances, but I had no choice; I had to get on with it.

It was 3:00am, and everywhere seemed dark, silent and lonely. When I arrived home I couldn't bear to go in the house. I simply sat in the car, totally and utterly drained and exhausted. The house looked dark, dreary and desolate, like an empty shell. It matched my mood. There was a vital presence missing: Mervyn's.

For the first time, I acknowledged what it would be like to have his presence missing in the future. An emptiness and feeling of utter desolation swept over me. It was an indescribable emotion. The reluctance to let go of the person I loved was really strong. My heart was battered, bruised and broken. How was I going to bear it?

I sat and wept. The past forty eight hours had taxed me to my limits. To watch a loved one suffer is the hardest experience of all.

However, I was to have a revelation. Mervyn could remember nothing about the past two days. I was amazed! He could not remember the doctor coming out to the house, nor the ambulance men arriving and his ride to the hospital. I was astonished. He had no idea of what he had gone through. This gave me such comfort. I saw this as God's mercy again. He had been gracious. Although Mervyn had suffered, he wasn't aware of it! I felt the whole situation had been a test on my faith, and I was the one who had to deal with the bad memories.

Moving Day Miracle

Moving day arrived, and I constantly fretted as I thought of Mervyn. He would be in a hospital miles away from our new home. This was not how we had planned it, yet I realised that it could have been so much worse. I thanked God that he had preserved Mervyn's life.

I locked the door of our old home for the last time. I remembered the day we had moved in; I was glad that I had not been able to see the future at that time. It would have spoiled the present.

Never had I dreamt that we would leave our home under these circumstances. It was so hard, yet there were so many precious memories - so many happy times. One day I would be able to smile through my tears. One day I would be able to give thanks to God for all I had enjoyed here, but for now I would trust Him through this dark and perplexing time.

But God was to do something unexpected again. Half way through the day, I was given encouraging news. Mervyn's consultant had arranged with the local hospice to admit him. As I travelled with the removal team to our new house, Mervyn travelled by ambulance to the hospice. This place was two miles away from our new home. How convenient was that! It was an amazing miracle of provision. God had provided a way for us to be brought together on the day that I moved house.

Now I could focus on getting our new home ready. I wanted to bring Mervyn home as soon as possible.

A Place of Abundance

I noticed a Psalm (Psalm 66:8-12) that Mervyn had recently marked in his small Gideon's Bible. My eyes picked out some of the lines he had emphasized:

Psalm 66:8-10

Let the whole world bless our God and loudly sing His praises.
Our lives are in His hands and He keeps our feet from stumbling.
You have tested us, O God; you have purified us like silver.

The final line that Mervyn had emphasized in verse twelve moved me to tears:

Psalm 66:12

We went through fire and flood, but you brought us to a place of great
abundance.

Yes, our faith had been tested through fire and flood. But through it all my Romans 8:28 rainbow had remained intact. Surprisingly, its seven comforting promises had become even more precious. Somehow, in some way, God would work to bring good out of our turmoil and pain.

I now had a huge question: would our new home be a place of great abundance for Mervyn or would his next move be to a heavenly place of even greater abundance?

Very soon I would be given the answer.

Chapter Eight

Final Journey

Luke 22:42

Father, if you are willing, remove this cup from me.
Nevertheless, not my will but yours be done.

A New Home

It felt strange waking up in new surroundings. The house creaked and vibrated in the strong wind. It would take time to become familiar with the different sounds.

I flinched as a flock of seagulls screeched loudly overhead, their haunting, evocative cries seemed to emphasize the emptiness and loneliness of the place. Tears flowed as a wave of sadness and nostalgia swept over me. I would never wake up in our old home again, and neither would Mervyn. We had both now crossed over into new territory. I would need to cling tightly to my Romans 8:28 rainbow of promises through the uncertain times ahead.

Idly I daydreamed. What must it be like to wake up and find that you are in heaven? How awesome! No-one would wake up there and feel sad or lonely - not after a 'welcome home' party arranged by Jesus and the angels! No unpacking or cleaning would be required either. Everything would be perfectly prepared and ready. More importantly, no one would wake up to find the place empty. I would be surrounded by loved ones who had gathered to greet me. The more I thought about it, the more I realised that heaven is the most abundant home anyone could wish to move into!

Some people think that heaven is full of fluffy clouds where angels sit in pyjamas playing harps! However, the Bible describes heaven as a place of indescribable beauty. It is the home that Jesus has promised to all who would believe in Him.

Death, the world's greatest preacher, has no place in heaven because in heaven...

Revelation 21:4b

...there will be no more death or sorrow or crying or pain. All these things are gone forever.

Paul, the apostle, in what we might term an 'out of body experience' saw the reality of heaven. He wrote:

2 Corinthians 12:4

But I do know that I was caught up to paradise and heard things so astounding that they cannot be expressed in words, things no human is allowed to tell.

The wonder of heaven enabled him to say:

Romans 8:18

Yet what we suffer now is nothing compared to the glory He will reveal to us later.

Paul suffered deeply because of His faith in Jesus, but he considered his sufferings as nothing compared to what awaited him in heaven. What an awesome vision God gave to him!

I wondered what Mervyn's first thought was as he awoke. It would be his first morning in the hospice. Was he too wondering about waking up one day and finding himself in heaven? He had talked about it a lot. We both had. It seemed surreal to think that as I was getting ready to welcome Mervyn to our earthly home, Jesus was also getting his heavenly home ready.

Jesus told His disciples:

John 14: 2-3

There is more than enough room in my Father's home. If this were not so, would I have told you that I am going to prepare a place for you? When everything is ready, I will come and get you, so that you will always be with me where I am.

I still continued to pray for the cancer to be destroyed though. I had no doubt that God could do this. He had mercifully answered my prayer when Mervyn's life had hung in the balance a few days ago. I would have been overwhelmed if I had needed to organise a funeral as well as a house move at the same time. God's kindness made me even more persistent and determined in the place of prayer.

I also prayed for strength and energy. I needed to prepare the house for Mervyn's arrival as I wanted to make the most of the time we had left together. The plan was that Mervyn would be released from the hospice as soon as the doctor arranged a better pain-controlling prescription.

Hospice

I had been startled by some of the reactions to Mervyn's move to the local hospice. Most comments were negative and spoken in a horrified whisper: "That's where people go to die," or "No one ever comes out alive when they go into a hospice." It's funny how people appear to forget that many patients also die in a hospital!

Entering a hospice for the first time was a strange experience. I wasn't sure what to expect. It wasn't pleasant to be visiting a place for terminally ill people. I felt tense and nervous. I had never seen anyone die, and I wasn't sure how I would react. The spectre of death seemed to be looming over me again. A prolonged terminal illness is a very different situation to a sudden death.

I was to be pleasantly surprised when I arrived at the reception. It was both warm and welcoming. The building was modern, well maintained and tastefully decorated and the grounds beautiful and well kept.

Mervyn was in a four-bedded ward where he could see the gardens from where he lay. He was keen to have some time outside, so I helped him into his wheelchair and wheeled him around the hospice grounds.

It was lovely to be able to take him outside in the fresh air and sunshine, but as I passed the different wards it seemed as if I had entered another world. I saw the handiwork of the world's best preacher, Death, everywhere. Cancer inflicts some terrible disfigurements and suffering. It is also no respecter of age. There were patients of all ages, young and old.

Shattering News

We were to have another blow. The hospice doctor arrived and discussed our situation with us. He explained that the twelve months prognosis was highly unlikely. The cancer was aggressive and spreading quickly. He wouldn't give an exact timescale, other than saying that the time left was short.

I was stunned. We had hoped and prayed for even longer than the twelve months prognosis. Not only that, we had just moved house into a new area away from friends and family!

It was devastating. Was this true? Would God take Mervyn home sooner rather than later? I couldn't think or speak; all I could do was stare dumbly at the doctor. He assured us he would do everything he could to arrange Mervyn's transfer home over the next week or two.

Mervyn took the news stoically. As far as he was concerned, the situation was in God's hands. He would go home to heaven when the time was right - although that didn't stop us hoping and praying for a miracle recovery too.

I have discovered that we have inner resources that are never tapped until we find ourselves in dire circumstances. God definitely gave me renewed physical energy. Two weeks of frenetic activity followed this news. The hospice delivered a special bed with a lifting hoist plus all the other paraphernalia needed to nurse a terminally ill person at home. I even made a wooden ramp for the wheelchair, although I have to admit it wobbled a bit!

The long awaited day when Mervyn would come home arrived. I was so excited! I looked forward to the ambulance bringing Mervyn to the house at 10:00am, but at breakfast time the telephone rang. My heart sank like a stone. Surely it would not be the hospice? Unfortunately, it was.

I was given the news that Mervyn would not be coming home that day. He had been sedated due to an excruciating spinal spasm. The hospice would not consider moving him under the circumstances. I was totally devastated.

Another time was arranged for the following week. I prayed constantly. Surely this time it would happen? It was important that Mervyn was moved before it was too late. Unbelievably, the same situation occurred and the ambulance cancelled. The hospice considered Mervyn too sick to be moved. Very gently the doctor warned me that Mervyn's time was running out.

Whether I liked it or not, I had to face the harsh truth. God had clearly given the answer to my question. God's bountiful place of abundance for Mervyn would be heaven. It would not be our new home. It was hard to think that he would end his days in the hospice. It still hurts. I regretted the fact that I had not arranged for him to come home immediately from the hospital, but moving house at such a difficult time exacerbated the situation. Neither of us anticipated his condition deteriorating so rapidly in the hospice.

Would I have coped at home? I really do not know, but my disappointment was like a painful sore that wouldn't heal until I accepted that some things just don't work out the way we want them to. We make decisions, believing that we are doing the right thing at the time. None of us can do any more than that.

I thought about how much life is similar to a journey. Like any journey there are times when the road is hard and painful. The plans we make can be thwarted by unexpected obstacles, but although a cloud temporarily hid my rainbow, through eyes of faith I knew that it was still there.

Last Hard Road

There should be a warning sign posted above Christians walking on the last stretch of road. "Be careful - this is Satan's last opportunity to derail your faith."

If things could get any worse, they did. Soon more complications arose. A painful infection started in Mervyn's elbow. It became larger than a tennis ball. It had to be lanced and drained every day - not a pleasant procedure. His lower back area was raw with open sores adding to his misery and discomfort. The radiotherapy treatment on that area had never healed and was steadily getting worse. It constantly distressed him, but the hardest part of it all was the indignity. He hated not being able to walk or do things for himself.

Although Mervyn's final mile was awful, it taught me so much. I was humbled as I witnessed the perseverance of his personal faith in Jesus. It was a privilege to be with someone whose faith never wavered despite having to endure so many traumas.

Mervyn told me he would be guided by a Scripture verse through his suffering:

1 Peter 4:19 (ESV)
Therefore let those who suffer according to God's will entrust their souls to a faithful Creator while doing good.

For him, faith meant we trust God with every detail of our own lives and those of our loved ones, no matter how tragic or senseless the situation.

A Heavenly Focus

The final time for Jesus was a hard road too. A false, trumped-up trial and cruel flogging were followed by the most horrific execution of all time - death by Roman crucifixion.

Jesus did not focus on the sufferings He was going through, however. He focused on achieving the free gift of eternal life for those who would believe in Him. He endured in order to return back home to His Father victorious over sin and death. He arose from His burial tomb to prove it.

Hebrews 12:1b-4b
Think of all the hostility He endured from sinful people; then you won't become weary and give up.

Jesus identifies with our fears about suffering. He understands because He suffered so much Himself.

Mervyn endured "all things" because of his focus. He simply looked up. He looked towards heaven with so much joy that it was infectious! He looked forward to seeing loved ones waiting in heaven; he talked about seeing his mother who had died a few years previously.

It dawned on me that entering heaven is also a time of great reunions! There is so much to look forward to. The reality of heaven makes all the difference when we have to bear the hardship of inexplicable experiences.

To endure watching someone you love suffer is agonizing. It tore me apart. It was definitely a test on my faith as well, but for the first time I realised that God understands and sympathises. In order to save the world, God had to allow His beloved Son to suffer horrendously. I had never considered how hard it must have been for God to endure watching Jesus suffer.

Why?

One of the questions most of us ask when something tragic happens is "Why?" Why did you allow this to happen Lord? Why so much suffering?

I asked Mervyn, "Why do you think this has happened to us? Why do you think you had to go through all this?"

He replied, "I don't ask why. Instead I ask why not. Why should it *not* happen to me? Why should it *not* happen to us? Did Jesus ever ask, 'Why should I have to die so others can live?' Did He ask, 'Why should I have to suffer when I did nothing wrong?'"

That response stumped me. It certainly wasn't what I expected!

He quoted the prayer of Jesus before His crucifixion:

Luke 22:42

Father, if you are willing, please take this cup of suffering away from me, yet I want your will to be done, not mine.

Of course Mervyn would have preferred things to be different, just as Jesus would have preferred a different way, but now he could really identify with the suffering Jesus went through on his account. He could fully appreciate that heart-wrenching prayer of Jesus! He was learning to pray with the same humble attitude: "Father, if you are willing, please heal this awful disease; yet I want your will to be done, not mine."

I saw, with awe, Mervyn trust God in a situation he didn't understand and not even ask a 'why'.

I wondered again about the Biblical story of Job's suffering. It reveals a spiritual battle going on behind everyday life. Satan challenges Job's reason for worshiping God. Satan taunts God's policies. He claims Job only serves God because everything in his life is good.

So God allows Job to be put on trial. Of course, Job is totally unaware of this! Tragedy after tragedy comes into Job's life. Finally, he suffers terrible health problems. All heaven watches as this drama unfolds... Will Job lose his faith in God? Will he continue to worship through so much suffering? Even Job's friends tell him that he must have sinned to have brought so much suffering on himself, but despite everything, Job holds on to his faith in God. It is an incredible story of endurance and loyalty.

Was there a spiritual battle going on behind Mervyn's suffering? I don't know, but what I do know is this: there is something amazing about faith that endures through prolonged suffering. It definitely glorifies God! In Hebrews 11 we read, in a long list of 'faith heroes', of supernatural deliverances. We also read of those who endured without supernatural deliverance. Both glorified God in different ways.

God's ways and thoughts are far above our ways (Isaiah 55: 8-9). We cannot expect to understand the reason why things happen the way they do. But God does not ask us to understand. He asks us to believe and trust in Him; that means through the tragic circumstances of our lives, not just the good! God's purposes are always enacted from an eternal standpoint.

I believe that in eternity we will understand the answers to all of our why's. But maybe when we get there we will be so enthralled with the glory of heaven that our why's will not seem important anymore!

Last Hymn

The last hymn Mervyn wrote emphasized how he wanted to spend whatever time he had left...

LET US WORSHIP YOU LORD

Let us worship you Lord, come and bow before you,
Let us worship you, while there's still time.
Listening for your voice Lord, speaking in the stillness,
Help us worship you, while there's still time.

Chorus:
We will worship you, while there's still time,
Cleanse our hearts and purify our minds.
We will worship you Lord, come and bow before you,
Help us worship you, while there's still time.

Let us worship you Lord, come and bow before you,
Let us worship you, while there's still time.
Trusting you for guidance, learning true obedience,
Help us worship you, while there's still time.

Let us worship you Lord, come and bow before you,
Let us worship you, while there's still time.
Learning from your word Lord, quickened by your Spirit,
Help us worship you, while there's still time.

Let us worship you Lord, as that day draws nearer,
All around we see the promised signs.
We would live for you Lord, walking by your power,
Help us worship you, while there's still time.

Chapter Nine

Home at Last

2 Corinthians 5:1

For we know that when this earthly tent we live in is taken down (that is, when we die and leave this earthly body), we will have a house in heaven, an eternal body made for us by God Himself and not by human hands.

Nightmare Nights

I normally arrived at the hospice at breakfast time and stayed until 9.30pm in the evening. The daytime staff were always caring and supportive. They fully involved me in Mervyn's daily routine and let me get on with the task of caring for him. It was a great arrangement because if I needed anything they did all they could to sort it out. Not only that, if Mervyn had an excruciating spasm he could be injected as quickly as possible. I acknowledged that this would have been difficult to handle at home on my own. In spite of this, however, an incident occurred which led me to decide to spend the nights at the hospice also.

Early one morning at about five thirty the telephone rang. I jerked awake from an exhausted sleep. It was Mervyn. He asked me to come immediately and he sounded distressed. I hurriedly dressed and dashed over to the hospice.

It appeared that he had had an altercation with a nurse on the night shift. It brought home his utter helplessness and vulnerability. For a man who had been strong, independent and forthright, his physical helplessness was scary. He was at the mercy of other people, their kindness or otherwise. It hit me like a thunderbolt. It seemed that Mervyn hated the nights. He had not said anything previously because he had not wanted me to be worried.

It wasn't easy staying at the hospice overnight. If ever I needed my Romans 8:28 rainbow of promises to shine over me it was then. It was a strange, depressive place at night: eerie and lonesome. The staff seemed to disappear into thin air. The sound of patients struggling to breathe seemed magnified in the silence as I tried to get some sleep on a recliner by Mervyn's bed. It was utterly hopeless.

It's funny how everything seemed to be twice as bad throughout the dark nights, despite the dim nightlights in the corridor. I used to long desperately for the first light of dawn to appear.

In the past I had heard people comment about experiencing a foretaste of hell in this life. I began to identify with those comments. The terrible thing about hell is that there is no dawn. The Bible describes it as a place of utter darkness and blackness (Jude 13 and Matthew 8:12).

Through those long, lonely, dark nights in the hospice, God gave me a glimpse of the horror of hell. It has been a powerful driving force in reaching out to others with the Good News of Jesus. Contrary to popular belief, God doesn't send anyone to hell. God has done everything possible through Jesus to make sure we don't go there. But if we refuse the offer of forgiveness for our sins provided through Jesus, we send ourselves there.

John 3:16

God loved the world so much that He gave His one and only Son, so that everyone who believes in Him will not perish but have eternal life.

Sowing in Tears

It was harrowing trying to get Mervyn comfortable. Some of the night staff were not very helpful or understanding. There were times when I almost lost my temper over their attitude. I felt taxed to the very limit - mentally, physically and emotionally - but the thought of Mervyn always spurred me on. I could not let him down now by collapsing with exhaustion. I had to rely on God to give me strength, moment by moment, through those long, dreary nights!

In the dim nightlight I sometimes browsed through the Psalms for comfort and inspiration. As I read through one Psalm, the conviction to publicly preach the Good News about Jesus was laid on my heart very clearly. Tears streamed down my face as I read it over and over:

Psalm 126:4-6

Restore our fortunes, Lord,
As streams renew the desert,
Those who plant in tears,
Will harvest with shouts of joy.
They weep as they go to plant their seed,
But they sing as they return with the harvest.

The first part was true for me. I would leave this place weeping. But I also believed that God was showing me that if I trusted Him despite my tears, He would reward me with a rich harvest. It was an incredible moment. I was to obey His call to plant the seed of the Gospel of Jesus in the hearts of men and women. He would open doors; I was to obey and go through them. The harvest I would one day reap would make me 'shout with joy', but I could not do anything without His enablement and anointing. I would need a powerful awareness of His presence with me.

Was the song 'Out of Egypt' going to inspire me in a way I had never anticipated or dreamed? If so, the words that Mervyn had written were prophetic: "Certainly [God] will go with [me], there's no need to fear or dread." God would give me everything I needed in Jesus. Jesus is enough!

Despite my personal distress, I did have some special times. I was asked to play a hymn on the organ for the wedding of a patient in the hospice chapel. It was 'Great is Thy Faithfulness'. Everyone had teary eyes during the service, and the Hospice Chaplain conducted it all with great sensitivity. He was just in time, as the groom died later that day. God had indeed been faithful!

Another occasion had a deep effect on me. I met with someone who had experienced an 'out of body' sensation. They described seeing a great light and hearing a voice call out their name. They believed it was the voice of Jesus speaking to them. They became aware of being outside of the building, on the rooftop, before returning to their body again.

I didn't know what to think, but I could see that it had transformed them from atheism. They now truly believed in an afterlife, in God and in Jesus. How could I disagree with such an experience? They asked me to share this story so that it might help others facing death.

I saw that I should never limit God's amazing grace. God may speak directly to people in their dreams or unconsciousness to give them another opportunity to put their faith in Him. He does not always speak through human messengers. He uses many different methods and ways to reveal Himself. His whole mission in sending Jesus was to save us from the consequences of sin.

2 Peter 3:9

He does not want anyone to be destroyed, but wants everyone to repent.

Final Days

"I just want to be with Jesus," Mervyn constantly said nearer the end. He wanted to be out of the body that was giving him so much grief.

2 Corinthians 5:8b

We would rather be away from these earthly bodies, for then we will be at home with the Lord.

Jesus had prayed:

John 17:24

Father, I want these whom you have given me to be with me where I am. Then they can see all the glory you gave me because you loved me even before the world began!

As Mervyn's weariness, pain and indignity increased, so did his desire and joy for his eternal home. I could understand why. There was no pleasure living in a body which gave him so much distress. Sometimes I would leave the room when he was moved. I could not bear to listen to his moans of utter agony. It felt as though a thousand knives were being plunged into my heart.

But Mervyn still had a smile. One nurse called it an "angelic smile". Another said he was an "angelic man". Even when he became unable to speak he would rub his head on my arm or the nurse's arms to communicate his gratitude. It was a gesture that always moved me and the nurses to tears. I knew exactly what he was saying: "Thank you."

Or was it "I love you"?

Final Words

The final words of someone who is dying stand out like rare and precious jewels. The things that Mervyn said will always be etched within my mind.

"Remember that Jesus is here. He will take me to heaven at the point of death. I don't want you to be afraid. Instead, focus on my arrival in heaven!"

"I love you more than ever for standing by me through all this."

"Don't be afraid of the future. Jesus has a plan for you. Our time together was just one chapter in life's book. You have more chapters to come. Enjoy them!"

"I have prayed for you. Follow Proverbs 3:5: 'Trust in the Lord with all your heart, do not depend on your own understanding. Seek His will in all you do, and He will show you which path to take.'"

"Don't do anything if in doubt. Pray, pray and pray. God will answer."

"Don't grieve; you know where I am."

"I'm glad it's me going first. You will cope much better!"

That last comment made me laugh! It made both of us laugh. I was not sure that it was true, but I was glad that it gave him some comfort.

Final Moment

Mervyn was deteriorating fast. I had never been so conscious of each precious moment nor the presence of Jesus.

Divine arms held me tightly.

Divine arms carried me.

Deuteronomy 33:27

The eternal God is your refuge and His everlasting arms are under you.

God was my comfort as I became distressed. Jesus had His arms beneath me, holding me up.

It is hard to explain, but in my spirit I went into another dimension. I knew with absolute certainty that Jesus was praying for me. I saw beyond the suffering and torment; I saw beyond earth's temporal scene. I had a glimpse of heaven within my spirit. Jesus revealed to me that He was getting ready to receive Mervyn into His presence in heaven!

Suddenly the Holy Spirit's convicting power overwhelmed me. I knelt down. I was filled with the utmost yearning, and it was profound. In my mind I was reminded of an Old Testament story of two prophets: Elijah and Elisha. I remembered the time when God was about to take

Elijah up to heaven in a whirlwind. Elijah would be transported into heaven without dying first! As Mervyn had said, when God's plan for your life is over, it is! There is nothing anyone can do to stop it. However, it was the conversation that these two men had together before they parted that I was to focus on.

2 Kings 2:9-10

"Tell me [Elisha], what I can do for you before I am taken away?" Elisha replied, "Please let me inherit a double share of your spirit and become your successor."

Elisha asked that Elijah's God-given spiritual abilities and privileges might continue to live through him.

It became crystal clear as to why this passage of Scripture was being highlighted to me by the Holy Spirit. I was to make a similar request to God before Mervyn died. In tears, I prayed.

"Lord, you are taking the best out of my life. I know you lent him to me for a season. Now I humbly bring the same request of Elisha's. Would you give me double of what you gave to Mervyn? I want a double portion of the Spirit you poured on him. I know that if you grant me this, I need not fear the future. I will have power to preach the Good News about Jesus wherever you open a door. Amen."

One of the nurses came through the privacy curtains. It was a nurse with whom Mervyn and I had developed a close relationship. Looking back, I can see that God sent the right person to be with me as the final moment of parting drew near. She gently warned me that Mervyn would soon be going.

I replied, "We say he's going, but in heaven they say he's coming! They are saying: 'Get ready to welcome him home!'"

If "there is joy in the presence of God's angels when even one sinner repents" (Luke 15:10), what is it like when a child of God enters heaven? The angels must put on a welcome home party that no event on earth could ever hope to match!

I stroked Mervyn's head; it was a struggle. It wasn't a peaceful death like some that I had witnessed in the hospice. It was a fight, but I knew that within Mervyn's heart there was a supernatural peace. Although nature was fighting its own fight with sickness and disease, the most important battle of all had been fought and won. Mervyn's faith had not been shaken. It had grown stronger.

I held him closely as I quietly sang the hymn he loved: 'How Great thou art'. The last verse was so moving:

> *When Christ shall come with shout of acclamation*
> *And take me home – what joy shall fill my heart!*
> *Then I shall bow in humble adoration*
> *And there proclaim, my God,*
> *How great thou art!*

Home At Last!

With one last shuddering gasp, his heart stopped beating. It was a heart that had bravely endured so much distress throughout his final days. Now it was all over. Hot tears coursed down my throat, and I whispered the words I believed with all my heart that Jesus was speaking to him. "Well done, good and faithful servant. Enter thou into the joy of thy Lord" (Matthew 25:23, NKJ). Mervyn was home at last!

Mervyn died in my arms at 4.42pm on 1st June 2005. Exactly six weeks after being transferred to the hospice, Mervyn was transferred to heaven.

It was a sacred and hallowed moment. Time appeared to be almost suspended. I felt as though my heart had stopped as well. The realisation that my world would never be the same again hit me like a giant tidal wave. I would never see him on this side of heaven again.

A deep desolation descended like a huge, black volcanic ash cloud. My heart strained with anguish. This parting was indescribable. Nothing had prepared me for this feeling of utter devastation. The final moment was like being cut in half. That is the only way I can describe it. Despite having known it would happen, my system jammed with shock. I trembled violently with distress as the awful reality of death sank in.

Mervyn had told me to remember Jesus would be with Him when he passed away, and as I stared at his vacated body, I realised Mervyn would be staring into the face of his beloved Saviour, Jesus Christ. It gave me tremendous comfort. He would be waking up to the reality of heaven! No need to try to imagine what it was like; he was there! Finally at home in the mansion prepared for him by Jesus. No more suffering, no more pain, no more crying, no more lonely nights of endurance. God had truly brought him to a place of great abundance.

The Psalmist wrote:

Psalm 30:5b

Weeping may last through the night, but joy comes with the morning .

Mervyn had endured a long night, but now his weeping was over. His joy was complete and his morning had broken in heaven.

For me though, the night of weeping had just begun. Would the seven promises in my Romans 8:28 rainbow be enough to take me through the ensuing months, even years, of grief and uncertainty? I had seen how a Christian man dies. Mervyn had finished his race with flying colours.

Could I take up the baton he had passed on to me? Could I follow the call that God had laid on my heart: to preach the Gospel? I wanted to with all my heart, but would my prayer for a double share of all that God had given to Mervyn be given to me? Who was I, that God would do such a thing?

I wept. Life suddenly seemed terrifying.

The Certainty of the Unexpected

Chapter Ten

Picking up the Pieces

Romans 8:35

Can anything ever separate us from Christ's love? Does it mean He no longer loves us if we have trouble or calamity, or are persecuted, or hungry or destitute, or in danger or threatened with death?

Everlasting Glue

"Stop it!" Two words cut across my grief like a razor blade. The voice of Jesus in my head continued. "You've still got me! Haven't I told you I will always be with you?"

I stopped weeping. I was astonished!

Jesus had spoken very powerfully to reassure me when I left the 'true way' group, but now He had given me something even more special to help me: my Romans 8:28 rainbow! Its promises kicked into action. Through weary, tear-stained eyes of faith I saw it shine above my storm. Divine love encircled me. The third promise glowed in glorious brilliance: *I had reassurance because God was certainly with me.* I was not alone. What a contrast to the dark, menacing thunder clouds of grief and despair!

Into my mind flowed the words of Mervyn's song 'Out of Egypt': "Certainly, I will go with you; there's no need to fear or dread." When Moses left Egypt, it was the beginning of a new life. He was given the task of leading God's people through a hostile wilderness to a fruitful land. He had to go through some extremely difficult experiences in the wilderness, but God was with him every step of the way. I felt as though I had suddenly entered a wilderness of my own. The future seemed daunting, but just as Moses experienced, God would be with me every step of the way. I would have to rely completely on God for guidance in the future, but as someone once said, "We can trust our unknown future to a known God!"

There is an Old Testament story of King David and his men. Returning home from the battlefield, they found their wives and children had been taken away as captives and their city destroyed.

1 Samuel 30:4

They wept until they could weep no more.

Worse still, David's men became bitter and blamed him for their loss. They even considered stoning him to death. But "David encouraged himself in the Lord His God" (1 Samuel 30:6b, NKJ). He didn't give up hope; he turned to God in his grief, distress and terror. God responded by turning a situation that looked hopeless into one of hope once more.

David's faith resulted in the people recovering everything that had been taken from them.

I saw something in this story that could be applied to my own situation. In distress we have a choice. We can either turn to God in our grief, pain and hopelessness or we can turn against Him. We can become bitter or we can become better. The future may not look very hopeful, but again, we have a choice. We can turn to God in our hopeless situation or we can turn away from Him. David's situation looked hopeless, but he took it to God and God gave him hope once more.

The second promise in my Romans 8:28 rainbow shone: *I had hope because with God no situation is hopeless!*

No matter how bad things looked to me, God could turn everything around in a way that would be beyond my greatest imagination. But I had to trust Him through my pain and grief. I decided that, even though nothing seemed to make sense, I would still trust God.

The Bible verse that Mervyn had given me to follow was challenging me again!

Proverbs 3:5b

Trust in the Lord with all your heart, do not depend on your own understanding.

If I could do this then God would help me pick up the broken pieces of my life to start over again.

On my kitchen table lay a cassette of worship songs. It had been given to me by a lovely Christian girl that I had met when moving into the area. The words that she had written on the cover suddenly arrested my attention: "May you draw close to God through these songs and feel His loving care being the glue that holds you together in the days that come."

Her words were prophetic. I suddenly knew I was being given reassurance again. Although I did not understand why Mervyn had been taken away from me, I could rest in the sanctuary of God's love for me. God's loving care would glue the broken pieces of my life back together again.

All through the Bible, God is constantly telling His people how much He loves them.

Jeremiah 31:3

I have loved you, my people, with an everlasting love. With unfailing love I have drawn you to myself.

God's love to me was like everlasting glue or supernatural loving glue. God's love isn't a love that is here today and gone tomorrow. It's everlasting! How strong is that! It is impossible to measure. It is glue that never fails or runs out. He would stick by me no matter what. Nothing could separate me from God's love - nothing at all!

Suddenly I felt joyful! The seventh promise in my Romans 8:28 rainbow shone out: *I had joy because God loves me!*

The apostle Paul wrote:

Romans 8:35

Can anything ever separate us from Christ's love? Does it mean He no longer loves us if we have trouble or calamity, or are persecuted, or hungry, or destitute, or in danger or threatened with death?

I love the answer that Paul wrote to his own question:

Romans 8:37-39

No, despite all these things, overwhelming victory is ours through Christ, who loved us and I am convinced that nothing can ever separate us from God's love. Neither death nor life, neither angels nor demons, neither our fears for today nor our worries about tomorrow – not even the powers of hell can separate us from God's love. No power in the sky above or in the earth below – indeed, nothing in all creation will ever be able to separate us from the love of God that is revealed in Christ Jesus our Lord.

One Priority

I decided that I wouldn't go to see Mervyn in the funeral home. I wanted the memory of his difficult death to fade in my mind. I believed that going would open up a wound that was very new and painful, but a conversation with a friend who had been bereaved changed my mind. She encouraged me to go as she believed I would regret it later on otherwise. I should not miss a final opportunity to say goodbye to someone I loved. She felt it would bring me peace - and how grateful I am that she did!

I chose to say my last farewell alone. I wanted to be able to concentrate solely on Mervyn. I also prayed that God would give me peace about his death. My heart beat rapidly with emotion as I went into the room where he was lying. It was a beautiful room, but I only had eyes for his casket. Part of me felt afraid of how he might look, but the other part longed to see him for the last time.

I approached hesitantly. He looked just like the Mervyn I knew and remembered before his illness had changed him! I wondered what I had been afraid of. His face was relaxed and calm as though he were simply asleep.

I was amazed to see that he was holding in his crossed hands one single red rose. I had bought red roses for him in the hospice! After all those restless, tormented nights and days he was finally at rest. Of course, there were now no more battles with pain! Futilely I wished that he could speak to me. It was surreal to see him so still and silent. I wanted to pray, "Get up out of your casket and live again!" but I knew he was no longer there. He was now with Jesus; he would not want to come back! He would be enthralled, looking around his abundant home in heaven with Jesus!

I related to what the Apostle Paul wrote about our physical bodies being the 'house' or 'tent' that our spirit (personality, mind, emotions) lives in. Like tenants in a house, we move out when our physical body or 'house' dies. The physical and spiritual literally part company!

Ecclesiastes 12:7

The dust will return to the earth and the spirit will return to God who gave it.

The physical body goes to sleep (dies) until the resurrection day (2 Corinthians 5:1-10 & 1 Corinthians 15:12-58), and the spirit returns to God.

My memory of Mervyn's face in death dimmed and was replaced with this expression of perfect peace. If only I could describe fully what that meant to me. God was giving me the gift of a last special memory moment. He was in control of everything, even when it didn't seem like it.

This experience showed me how much He cared about my pain and confusion. The fourth promise in my Romans 8:28 rainbow shone out: *I had peace because God was in control!*

As I stood beside his casket, peace flowed through me and pervaded my being. I felt a complete stillness and quietness that was awesome. Time seemed to stop, and the presence of God through the Holy Spirit filled the room. There are moments in life that can never be erased from our memory, and this was one of them. God was speaking to me directly and impressing His will on my mind. I was to be a testament of His amazing grace through Jesus, and He would open up the doors of opportunity.

I remained perfectly still. I never wanted to leave that room or even move again. It was absolutely incredible. I bowed my head and worshipped. Beside Mervyn's open casket, I surrendered my life, my heart and my all to God. It was clear; God was going to turn around all that had happened to reach others with the Good News of Jesus. Mervyn's death was going to be used to glorify God. I didn't know how, where or when, but it would be revealed to me as I continued to trust Him.

The first promise of my Romans 8:28 rainbow glowed magnificently over Mervyn's casket: *I had comfort because God would work "all things" for my eternal good!* Mervyn's prophecy regarding Romans 8:28 was speaking to me in a way I had never thought possible.

From this moment on I was to have:

One priority
One purpose
One plan
One prayer
One principle
One power
One passion

...to go and proclaim the Good News (or Gospel story) about Jesus.

An idea came to me. It startled me in its pure audacity! I was to speak about Jesus at Mervyn's funeral. Immediately I was full of doubt. How could I do that? I had never spoken publicly before. I certainly did not feel able to do that under the current circumstances. I was completely and utterly exhausted. But the voice of God persisted. No matter how hard I tried to ignore His convicting power, it just became stronger. I continued to resist, giving myself a host of various excuses ranging from tiredness to not knowing what I would say, but God gave clear direction.

The first direction was sensible. He said, "Go home and get some rest."

The second was, "I will anoint your lips and speak through you."

The third was, "I thought you said you trusted me..."

As I left the room, the Funeral Director was hovering anxiously outside. He looked astonished when I smiled composedly at him. I suppose he had been wondering if I had collapsed, since I had taken so long! I told him about our faith in Jesus and why I could smile despite my sorrow. He was amazed but seemed to appreciate the experience of knowing me. He said that it was very different from the reactions he usually had to deal with.

God had spoken; that was all that mattered. He was certainly with me. What an amazing day! What an amazing rainbow created especially for me!

First Speaking Engagement

The day of Mervyn's funeral dawned. The service was held in an unusual, white-washed, wooden church building on the burial grounds. Mervyn would have loved it. It reminded me of churches built on the Bible Belt in America. Inside were the old-fashioned pew benches.

I was incredibly nervous about what now lay ahead. Before leaving the house, I impulsively decided to take one of Mervyn's sleeping tablets to calm myself down. Just as quickly I spat it out! Choking and spluttering over the sink, I suddenly panicked. What if I fell asleep in the service? What would people think? I had to see the humorous side of it even though I felt as though I were falling to pieces.

I knelt and prayed.

"Father God, you see me. You see how ridiculously I am behaving. Please help me to do this last thing for Mervyn and to obey your call. But I can only speak if you anoint and enable me. In Jesus' name, help me! Amen."

My 'everlasting loving glue' was powerful. When the time came for me to go to the front and speak, a peace descended over me. God's loving presence held me together. It was an incredible experience of God's enablement and empowerment. I had to rely totally on God. Here is a small extract of what I said:

> *Throughout Mervyn's illness and my house move to this area, there were two questions that we frequently asked each other. Mervyn's was 'Are you ready to move?' and mine was 'When will you be ready to come home?' As Mervyn's pain developed rapidly, we soon realised that Mervyn's next move would not be to a temporary dwelling place on earth. God was giving him notice that his next move would be to his final and permanent destination. The body that Mervyn lived in - or his 'house' - was becoming an unpleasant dwelling place.*

> *He began to be eager to move out of his earthly house because the promise to believers in Jesus is that when we leave our home in the body we are immediately in the presence of the Lord. 'So we are always full of courage, we know that as long as we are at home in the body we are away from the Lord's home. For our life is a matter of faith, not of sight. We are full of courage and would much prefer to leave our home in the body and be at home with the Lord'.[4]*

> *The Bible tells us that one day all of us will move on from this earth to a permanent place. It tells us that there are only two places or destinations we can go to after death – heaven or hell – and that our final destination is determined by our acceptance or rejection of Jesus Christ. We do not have an automatic right into heaven because the Bible states "for everyone has sinned"[5] and "no one is righteous, no not one".[6] Our good works alone are never enough to gain God's approval.*

---

[4] 2 Corinthians 5:6-8 (GNB)
[5] Romans 3:23a
[6] Romans 3:10

Mervyn questioned as a child how his sins could be forgiven in order that he could be assured of a home one day in heaven. He accepted and believed that Jesus paid the price required to take sinners to heaven. 'Anyone who believes in God's Son has eternal life.'[7] Not 'maybe' or 'might have', but 'already in possession of'.

To believe is to repent of your sin, recognise your personal need of forgiveness and to acknowledge that only the death of Christ can meet that need. The choice Mervyn made to do this has determined his eternal destiny today.

Mervyn loved John 14:2 in which Jesus told his followers that he was going ahead to prepare a place or a home for them. Jesus said, 'I go to prepare a place for you that where I am, there you may be also.' Whilst I had been preparing to welcome Mervyn to our new earthly home, Jesus had made his heavenly home ready. The Bible tells us: 'eye hath not seen, nor ear heard, neither have entered into the heart of man the things which God hath prepared for them that love him'.[8] In other words, our human minds cannot imagine or comprehend the beauty of our heavenly home.

As time went on, those two questions we both asked have been answered in a way neither of us expected, but Mervyn's final answer was, 'Yes, Jesus, I'm ready. I want to be home with you.'

Is death scary? Yes, but not if it means going home to be with Jesus.

Stunned, I sat down. I had done it! God had enabled me. The fifth promise in my Romans 8:28 rainbow glowed: *I had purpose because God had a plan for me.* There was not a whisper of doubt; God's plan for me was clear. I was to preach the Good News of Jesus. It was my purpose in life for the future.

What would Mervyn have thought about this experience? He had prayed that I would reach many people with the story of God's amazing grace through Jesus. He probably wouldn't have been surprised. He would have been incredibly moved at the way God was answering his prayers.

---

[7] John 3:36
[8] 1 Cor: 2:9 (ESV)

I looked at the red roses that covered Mervyn's casket. On the card, I had written:

A Rare and Beautiful Gentleman

The words 'rare and beautiful' I had copied from the verse that Mervyn had written when he had sent me an orchid. It was a description that fitted him perfectly. I wanted to give back something he had given to me. Of course, no one that day would have understood the significance of this, but he would have done.

At his burial place I was overwhelmed by emotion once more. This was what it felt like to be utterly heartbroken and devastated. I felt so much pain yet I also felt numb and empty. What a contradiction - tears of sorrow intermingled with those of joy! At my friend Annabel's funeral, so many years ago, I had not understood the gift of God's grace in Jesus, but God had chosen to reveal it to me.

The sixth promise in my Romans 8:28 rainbow shone through the mist of my tears: *I had blessing because God had chosen me!* How awesome to know that God has chosen to save us by His grace through faith in Jesus!

Second Spiritual Milestone

Mervyn's grave is my second spiritual milestone. It is sacred ground to me. Engraved on his tombstone is the epitaph "With Jesus." It explains where he is now in a very simple yet profound way. Without fail, my Romans 8:28 rainbow of promises shines vividly on that spot. I don't understand why things had to happen the way they did or why I had to lose him so soon, but I rest in what I do know. God wants me to trust Him.

I love the quote of Frederick W. Faber:

Darkness to the intellect,
But sunshine to the heart.

In the darkness of suffering and tragedy I believe it sums up my rainbow perfectly.

Grief's Aftermath

I treasured the words on a card that a dear friend sent me:

Thank you, dear Jesus,
For all that you have given me,
For all that you have taken from me,
For all that you have left me.

- St Thomas More, In the Tower

On the back, she had written:

We should console ourselves with the reality that there is no better reward
than to be loved as Mervyn loves you (and you him). How much richer
your life has been with him and how diminished your life would have been
without him in it. You are so very lucky to have experienced such love. I
urge you to hold on to these thoughts in the days ahead.

With my love as always, your friend,

Margaret.

"Life goes on" is a common - but true - expression. Life does indeed
go on, but the journey through grief is a difficult process. I do not think
that there is an easy way, but if there is then I didn't find it and no-one
told me about it! It is something that I had to journey through with God
by my side. There were many ups and downs along the way. I don't think
that grief ever goes away completely; it is not able to. Memories that have
been so precious cannot be deleted or instantly discarded from our minds.
It is simply that in time we are able to adjust to a new way of living
without that person. For me it was learning to live as a single person once
again. The loss of companionship and fun left a huge gap. Learning to do
things on my own and visiting places on my own seemed to highlight my
loss at first, but gradually it became easier.

A friend described my journey in grief as like being in a wilderness
place. They got it absolutely right - it is. It is a place that no one wants to

visit, but there is no choice about it. Unfortunately, it is a part of life in this world. Sooner or later, grief and loss will affect every one of us.

Grief has changed me; it has made my life richer in a way that I never thought would be possible. It has taught me a great deal. It is a journey that has shaped me to become the person that I am today. It has definitely made me a more compassionate and understanding person. The old expression "It's better felt than telt (told)" is brutally true. Even though grief has profoundly affected my journey in life, it has taught me how precious life, love and friendships are.

I have become all too aware of the brokenness in life around me: broken hopes, broken health, broken bodies, broken dreams, broken hearts, broken marriages, broken relationships, broken minds and broken spirits.

Grief has stirred within me to reach out to others who are hurting as well. It has enabled me to reach out across a divide of culture, race and religion, to a hurting world. I want to share with others the comfort God has given me. Grief has given me a tremendous passion to share my Romans 8:28 rainbow of comforting promises wherever I go.

Moving On

It was time to move on and pick up the pieces of my life again. There was much to do as I settled into a new area and house. There were death legalities such as probate to be obtained. At times it was overwhelming. I also had to sort out Mervyn's belongings. This was a very painful and emotional task but also unexpectedly cathartic.

Mervyn's large Bible was very precious to me. He also had a little burgundy-coloured Gideon's pocket Bible of the New Testament and Psalms. He carried this everywhere with him; it had been presented to him by the Gideon's organisation who had visited his school when he was just fourteen years old.

I found it in his belongings that were returned from the hospice. I eagerly leafed through its dog-eared pages. He had highlighted his favourite passages. This little Bible had been his constant companion since childhood and his encouragement throughout his illness and death. I was thrilled to find some notes he had shakily written at the back during his illness:

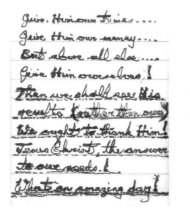

I call them Mervyn's guidance notes! Although they had not been written for me I felt as if they had! As I looked at the second page of notes, I knew that the key to everything in my life for the future was simple: I was to give everything I had to Jesus. Then, as Mervyn had written, "We shall see His results (rather than ours)!"

I was thrilled to find these notes. How precious to have something written that filled me with hope and inspiration! The first line was obviously what Mervyn considered a priority:

Matthew 6:33 (ESV)
Seek first the kingdom of God and His righteousness and all these things will be added to you.

If I would put God's business first then the promise was that He would take care of my business!

The second line was taken from Philippians:

Philippians 3:13b
Forgetting the past and looking forward to what lies ahead.

Very appropriate advice for my situation.

The third line was taken from an old hymn. [9]

Take my life and let it be
Consecrated Lord to Thee.

To consecrate something is to set it apart for a specific purpose or use. The Bible is full of examples of how God honoured individuals who consecrated their lives for His use. How amazing that Mervyn had written this. All I wanted to do now was to consecrate my life to God for His sole use and purpose.

I was awestruck when I saw how this led perfectly into the next point: "those that honour me!" This was taken from John 12:

John 12:26 (ESV)
If anyone serves me, the Father will honour Him.

God promised to honour those who served or lived to please Jesus! This meant that God would bless my service and ministry!

The final note was "...all things are possible." How appropriate! I never thought that I would write a book yet here I am writing one. This note was taken from Mark 9 and 10:

Mark 9:23
All things are possible, only believe.

Mark 10:27
All things are possible with God.

I must remember this when things seem impossible or problems insurmountable. God can turn around situations and circumstances in the blink of an eye. The Bible is full of awesome illustrations of God's power - from David slaying the giant Goliath to Jonah being swallowed by a whale. I prayed that my faith would increase to epic proportions so that God's power could flow through me. I also wanted a faith that could demolish the mountains of fear, doubt, disbelief, dismay and discouragement in an instant.

---

[9] 'Take My Life' by F.R.Havergal

Leaving a Legacy

For the first time, I appreciated how significant the things we leave behind us can be. These 'guidance' notes were like a priceless legacy! They were worth nothing in a material sense but invaluable in the light of eternity.

Suddenly a thought struck me. Mervyn had not only left notes behind as a legacy, he had left me! In a powerful way he had invested so much of his life into helping me appreciate all that I had in Jesus. A legacy only comes into effect after a death and it is left to benefit others. A pivotal moment in my life had been when he had laid down his armour and passed the torch of faith to me, but if I was to be an effective legacy and benefit others, I would need to be:

A Responsible Legacy
A Faithful Legacy
A Fearless Legacy
An Unchanging Legacy
A Passionate Legacy
A Prayerful Legacy
A Loving Legacy

The list that naturally flowed was a legacy of seven parts - God's perfect number. I began to get excited. Each part fitted perfectly together with the seven promises in my Romans 8:28 rainbow! This was no coincidence; I knew that God was going to help me become an effective legacy for His glory.

There was a condition attached, however. I had to continue living by faith under my rainbow of promises. To be an effective legacy, I would have to hold on to God's promises throughout all kinds of storms. I must never give in to the storms of fear, discouragement, ridicule or opposition. Only then would I become truly effective!

The Certainty of the Unexpected

Chapter Eleven

A Living Legacy

Acts 20:24

But my life is worth nothing to me unless I use it for finishing the work assigned me by the Lord Jesus — the work of telling others the Good News about the wonderful grace of God.

The Future

The date on my calendar currently shows the date of my wedding anniversary. It seems significant that I begin this chapter on that day. I feel as though I have now come full circle. I began this book remembering a day that changed my life forever. I now near the end of my story reflecting on another special time that changed my life forever. It was a day when I started out on a new path in life, not knowing where it would take me.

Without a doubt, one thing is abundantly clear: I have changed so much since those early days that I hardly recognise myself. The fear and timidity that made my life miserable has disappeared. I am astounded at how much God has transformed me. I see that despite my difficult experiences, God in His infinite grace has done a work in my heart and life that is truly amazing. I do, of course, recognise that there is much to be done. I am still an unfinished piece of work!

As the memories of that special day flood back, I thank God that He hides the future from our view. If I had known all that was ahead of me I would have found it hard to enjoy my life in the present. For the first time I ask myself, "If I had known the future, would I have made the same decisions?" The answer to that is a resounding "Yes!"

God's gift of a person into my life is something I cannot thank Him enough for. The effect and influence of Mervyn's life has dramatically impacted me forever. I can never go back to being the person I was when we first met. I certainly have no desire to do that. Mervyn played a huge role in building up my faith in Jesus in a tremendous way. I suppose that is why I see myself as his 'living legacy'.

I love the chorus of one of the songs I chose for Mervyn's funeral called "Because He (Jesus) Lives", written by Gloria and William J Gaither:

> *Because He lives, I can face tomorrow.*
> *Because He lives, all fear is gone.*
> *Because I know He holds the future*
> *And life is worth the living, just because He lives.*

Even though I do not know what my future holds, it doesn't matter. I know the one who does: Jesus! Because of that, life is definitely worth living, despite pain and bereavement. Jesus is alive! He is watching over me as I write this chapter just as He watches over Mervyn in heaven. That is so comforting and amazing.

I love Paul's letter of comfort to the Thessalonian church:

1 Thessalonians 4:13-14

Now dear brothers and sisters, we want you to know what will happen to the believers who have died so you will not grieve like people who have no hope. For since we believe that Jesus died and was raised to life again, we also believe that when Jesus returns, God will bring back with Him the believers who have died.

What an amazing reunion that will be! He continues:

1 Thessalonians 4:17-18

Then, together with them, we who are still alive and remain on the earth will be caught up in the clouds to meet the Lord in the air. Then we will be with the Lord forever. So encourage each other with these words.

This promise is exhilarating; it should thoroughly gladden and provide solace to aching hearts. Bereavement is a temporary situation!

The Impossible Becomes Possible

Shortly after Mervyn's death, I was hit by a double tsunami! Unbelievably, both of my parents were diagnosed with cancer at the same time. The prognosis for Mum was uncertain, so there was hope of a recovery; however, my father's prognosis was of terminal liver cancer, so there was none. He took the news stoically though. He believed that he had had a "good run", as he put it.

I was devastated that I could lose both my parents at the same time so soon after losing Mervyn, but although I felt overwhelmed I looked to my rainbow to find peace in this sudden and unpredictable maelstrom. Its promises reminded me that God was in control.

I wanted to find a way to speak to Dad about the need to be prepared for heaven. Even though the 'true way' religion did not use CDs or tapes, I felt drawn to look through Mervyn's collection of hymn tapes and CDs to find something appropriate. Unbelievably, the first tape I looked at was called 'Looking Homeward'. It was a collection of hymns compiled by Ruth Bell Graham (Dr. Billy Graham's wife) for her dying mother. This was perfect! I prayed that Dad would agree to listen to them on my portable player. He loved music, so it was possible that he would, and I was thrilled when he did!

On the tape cover, Mrs Graham had written:

Now that she is there (in heaven), I know nothing that would give her more joy than knowing these same hymns are ministering to all of us who are looking homeward.

Since the tape was compiled, Ruth Bell Graham has joined her mother in heaven. I am sure that both of them would be overjoyed to know how much pleasure these old hymns gave to my dad. It shows that we can even leave a powerful legacy behind us in a simple tape.

My father listened to these hymns with tears running down his cheeks. They were ministering to him and reaching him in a way I couldn't. I was always careful in my approach as he would never talk about anything spiritual with me. There was a barrier firmly in place that I simply could not break down, but I was astonished when he said that he believed Mervyn was singing to him from heaven through that tape.

It had a powerful effect on him. When I tried to explain that it was a tape of songs of different singers, he refused to believe me. I decided not to argue. I was more than happy that he was agreeing to listen to them. What did it matter if he thought it was Mervyn? I felt as though I was watching a miracle take place through this beautiful collection of songs. I was being shown again how God can do unexpected things when we least expect it.

A week before my father died, God worked another miracle. I was sad that I had always been unable to discuss eternal issues with him. I knew that I would have to simply trust God with this situation. When I tried to talk about such things, my father would become intransigent and refer to the 'true way' group as being the only true way left on the earth.

As I sat beside his bed, he suddenly opened his eyes. He told me how much he loved his Bible. For a moment I could not say anything. This was the first time he had ever voluntarily shared something spiritual with me. I was stunned! I then had a flash of inspiration and quickly asked if he would like me to read something from his Bible to him. Imagine my delight when he agreed!

For two whole hours we had a Bible study. He listened like a humble child (which was very unusual) as the Holy Spirit worked a transformation before me. We discussed John 3:16:

John 3:16

For God loved the world so much that He gave His one and only Son, so that everyone who believes in Him will not perish but have eternal life.

This verse gave Dad a deep peace and contentment. I explained that through repentance and faith in Jesus, our sins had been forgiven. God had saved us through grace as we put our trust in Jesus. Jesus is the person who has done all that is necessary to secure our entrance into heaven.

I read the story of the dying thief on the cross who turned to Jesus in repentance before He died and how Jesus promised this man that he would be with him in Paradise (heaven) after death (Luke 23:32-43). My father loved this story.

The impossible had become possible! It reminded me of God's encouragement to Moses:

Exodus 14:13-14

Fear not, stand firm, and see the salvation of the Lord, which He will work for you today. For the Egyptians whom you see today, you shall never see again. The Lord will fight for you and you have only to be silent.

I discovered there is a huge amount of Scripture that you can get through in two hours.

Inside the cover of his Bible my father had written, "Jesus is the silent listener to our every conversation." Jesus was more than listening that day. He had guided the conversation.

The time flew past as I "stood still and saw the salvation of the Lord, which He worked for me that day." That was my last conversation with my father before he died a week later, but through my tears I had peace and joy. After all those years, God had answered my prayer in a most unexpected way.

Eternal Investments

I read in the Old Testament of a King named Jehoram who was forty years old when he died. In the brief account of his life it says that...

2 Chronicles 21:20
Jehoram was thirty two years old when he became king and he reigned in Jerusalem eight years. He passed away, to no-one's regret.

These few words paint a depressing picture of the useless life that Jehoram lived. There was nothing good recorded about it. I certainly did not want to leave a legacy like that. As King he could have done so much to benefit others. What a waste of a tremendous opportunity in such a position.

I was challenged again by Mervyn's guidance notes. The first note had advised me to seek the interests of God's kingdom first. Jesus had said:

Matthew 6:19-21
Don't store up treasures here on earth, where moths eat them and rust destroys them, and where thieves break in and steal. Store your treasures in heaven, where moths and rust cannot destroy and thieves do not break in and steal. Where your treasure is, there the desires of your heart will also be.

I saw that whatever I set my heart upon would affect how I spent my time. I could spend time in activities that would amount to nothing in eternity, or I could work hard at building up something that would count as a valuable investment when I died.

What I focused my heart and mind on would determine the course of my life, my actions and attitudes. It would determine where I went, what I did and what I pursued. I wanted to leave a legacy that would point others to Jesus. I wanted to be used to bring eternal life and hope to others. Investing my time and energy this way would store up the eternal treasure that Jesus applauded. It was far superior to any earthly investments which are temporary and transitory.

One of the ways I wished to invest my time usefully was to become a volunteer member of a multi-faith hospital chaplaincy team. I loved every bit of the training and mentoring process and remember vividly the day I was allowed to go 'solo'.

My first assignment had been to find someone's false teeth! There is a practical side to this ministry as well as spiritual and emotional, but it is a ministry that has taught me much about the courage and fortitude of some amazing people that I have been privileged to meet.

Invariably, I always have what I call "God moments" when I visit. I have been amazed at how my own experience of grief and bereavement is used over and over to comfort and help others going through a similar journey.

Bad Things

One thing I do have great regret about is that I wasted so much time in the 'true way' religion, but even in that God showed me a special promise:

Joel 2:25 (ESV)
I will restore to you the years that the swarming locust has eaten.

Did this mean I was going to have some extra years added to my life and live to be a hundred and ten, or did it mean the quality of the years allotted to me would be incredibly fulfilling? I was not sure what to think, but what I am sure about is that where I have been broken down by the pressure of religion, God has built me up again to live a meaningful life. God is the expert restorer and renovator. I am living proof of that.

Bad things happen because of the choices we make. That is certainly one aspect, but God is more than able to turn around our circumstances in ways we could never imagine. He doesn't want us to live a life dragged down by remorse for our past or decisions we wish that we had never made. Our messed-up lives in His capable hands can be transformed far beyond our wildest dreams. However, He wants us to choose to come to Him with our pain, heartache and brokenness. God never pushes or forces us against our will.

The parable of the Prodigal Son returning home graphically demonstrates the tender heart of our heavenly Father (Luke 15:11-31). In this story the son finds to his amazement that even though he is still a long way from home, his father sees him and runs to meet him with outstretched arms. As the son stutters out his sorrow at his sin and rebellion, he discovers that he is not just forgiven but he is also restored back to being a cherished member of his father's household. It doesn't stop there either. His father throws a fabulous party to celebrate his son's return and gives him the finest robe, sandals and ring he can find.

A ring, in this period of Biblical history, was a symbol of authority. Like the robe, it indicated his renewed status as son and heir. No-one can doubt God's love for us in that story. It illustrates movingly that no matter where we have been or what we have done, there is an open welcome when we return with an attitude of repentance.

The Lord Jesus is the expert potter. Depending on our attitude, we are clay that He can remodel and remake into an amazing vessel to glorify Him. The difficulty for us is to believe that He can do what seems impossible. In faith we have to give Him all the broken pieces, the disappointments and hurts and all the misshapen bits of our lives.

Most of us have experienced some kind of bad thing in our lives. The list is endless: sickness; bereavement; divorce; betrayal; any kind of trauma that damages us physically, mentally or emotionally; but we have to be willing to submit to His workmanship and let Him put us back together again His way. That can be difficult if we have our mind set on our own desires and plans. It is impossible if we demand explanations before we agree to submit and trust our situation to God. This is because...

Hebrews 11:6

It is impossible to please God without faith. Anyone who wants to come to Him must believe that God exists and that He rewards those who sincerely seek Him.

Bad things can happen to us due to the choices that others make. This is often difficult to accept. It seems unfair and wrong that we have to live with the consequences of someone else's wicked or violent behaviour. It doesn't seem right when a good person suffers at the hands of an evil person or a good person becomes sick. My own sense of justice wants all the bad, evil people to suffer and die young - not someone I love and who is good - but as I look around, the harsh reality is that no-one can escape bad things happening to them. We live in a sin-sick world where the consequences of evil in society touch every one of us in so many different ways.

I identify with the Prophet Habakkuk in the Old Testament. He was greatly distressed by the wickedness and suffering he saw taking place around him. He could not understand why God did not intervene to stop it happening. His heart's cry is reflected in the opening chapter:

Habakkuk 1:1-3

How long, O Lord, must I call for help? But you do not listen! Violence is everywhere! I cry, but you do not come to save. Must I forever see these evil deeds? Why must I watch all this misery? Wherever I look I see destruction and violence.

Human nature, corrupted by sin's influence, has not changed through the centuries. It is still the same in the 21st century as it was in Habakkuk's time.

Habakkuk was perplexed and puzzled by God's apparent silence and lack of intervention, but when God eventually replied, he could not understand that either. However, when Habakkuk stopped focusing on trying to understand what God was doing and reflected instead on God's character, his perspective altered. His faith in God's power and intervention in the past raised his hopes for the future. As he started to dwell on God's character, he realised that what he did not understand could be left safely in God's hands.

To Habakkuk's surprise God challenged his faith:

Habakkuk 2:4 (ESV)

Behold, he whose soul is not upright in him shall fall, but the righteous shall live by his faith.

God does not want us to live a life dependent on having good circumstances or to worship Him because we have all the answers. Nor does He want us to worship Him because we have everything the way we want. No, He wants us to live by faith and trust in His character. He wants us to live our lives dependent on Him, yet He does not ask us to live resting on a blind faith. We live with faith in a God who has acted in history and has done a merciful work of grace for us through His Son, Jesus. He is a God who has promised to act in the future. At the right time God will intervene in history and change things from bad to good forever.

Although the problems remained and the pressures continued, as Habakkuk focused on God's character there was a strengthening of the inner man that made his heart rejoice. He burst into a song of praise.

Habakkuk 3:17-19

Even though the fig trees have no blossoms, and there are no grapes on the vines; even though the olive crop fails, and the fields lie empty and barren; even though the flocks die in the fields, and the cattle barns are empty, yet I will rejoice in the Lord! I will be joyful in the God of my salvation! The Sovereign Lord is my strength! He makes me as surefooted as a deer, able to tread upon the heights.

'Attitude' - Not Answers

Habakkuk's song of praise has become mine. Even though I don't have everything I would long to have in life, even though the pressures mount and my life is turbulent, I have a future to look forward to. One day God has promised to put everything right when sin's evil influence and power will be banished forever. It has helped me come to one conclusion as I draw near to the end of this book. It is one I intend to live by: "I don't have answers, I have attitude".

That attitude is simple. It is the one found in Proverbs 3:5-6.

Proverbs 3:5-6

Trust in the Lord with all your heart; do not depend on your own understanding. Seek His will in all you do and He will show you which path to take.

It does not make sense to me that God would take Mervyn so soon and in the way He did, but I have decided that I can trust God with all that I cannot understand. With this attitude, God can use me over and over again, no matter what happens, for His glory.

Good Things from Bad?

So can anything good come out of bad things? I cannot change the bad things that have happened to me. Neither can I transform bad situations into good situations, but I can now truly say that God can bring good out of bad when we trust Him. My own experiences of bad things have been used in so many ways to comfort and inspire others to turn to God also. A true way of measuring whether anything good has come out of my painful experiences in life is to ask those around me.

Do the listeners of the different events I am invited to speak at receive anything helpful or inspirational? Will the readers of this book find anything in its contents to help and encourage them to trust God through the tough times? The question as to whether anything good has come out of the bad things in my life or not is really for others to answer.

Compassion (Children in Poverty)

I currently sponsor two boys through 'Compassion'. Compassion is a ministry that works to "release children from poverty in Jesus' name". Their brochure explains:

Compassion works exclusively through local churches in developing countries and uses their intimate knowledge of people on the ground to identify and provide long-term support for children suffering the greatest need. Children attend a Compassion programme, regardless of their faith or background.

Mervyn had desired to help children in poverty. He could not stand to see a child suffer. He had a dream that maybe one day he would have enough money to buy a big, old house and fill it with orphan children or children who felt no one would love because they were disabled. It was one thing in life that he regretted not being able to do.

In the hospice, he asked me to arrange to sponsor a child before he died and urged me to try to do more in the future. I hope to contribute 25% of any royalties this book produces to Compassion. It would be a fantastic way to honour his memory and last request.

The two boys that I sponsor are currently aged eleven and twelve years old. I love the letters that I receive and the colourful drawings they create. I stick these on my fridge and have built up quite a collection over the past few years. They share all they have learnt about Jesus and how much it means to know that He loves them too. I am thrilled to play a small part in their lives, and I treasure the Bible verses they pick out for me. I also sponsor a girl in Malawi through Every Child.

More details about Compassion can be found at the back of this book. One thing is certain - anyone who decides to sponsor a child will receive a lot of love and be richly blessed in return.

Love and Loyalty

God knows how much I miss all that He has taken from me, but He allows our love and loyalty to be tested. When we remain loyal to God, despite life's traumas and storms, our worship becomes more precious to Him. We prove our love by being loyal. God has feelings too. He wants to be loved for who He is - His character - not for what we can get out of Him. He created us because He loved to do so. There was no one more devastated than God when our first parents, Adam and Eve, were disloyal to Him.

God created us with the freedom to choose. He did not want robots that would automatically conform or perform. God wanted us to respond to Him by worshipping Him from a heart of love, loyalty and faithfulness. Most of us would want to be loved like that too. His great love allows us to be free to make our own decisions about Him. We can either choose to respond to God's love and enter into a personal, intimate relationship with Him or we can choose to turn our backs on God and go our own independent way.

We can demand obedience - we can force and control others through fear - but we cannot demand or force love. Love is purely voluntary. That is why it is so special. Love is even more special if you know it has been loyal under stress and temptation. I suppose that's the proof of true love. "God is love" (1 John 4:8b) and He wants to be loved in a loyal way.

Rainbow Legacy

One unexpected thing God has given me is my rainbow of seven promises. The rainbow God created for Noah was also a legacy to benefit his descendants. It would be wonderful if my rainbow's seven promises could become a good thing to benefit others - a legacy I could leave behind me. Mervyn would be stunned to see the result of his faith in God's promise in Romans 8:28.

I saw how my seven legacy characteristics combined perfectly with my rainbow of promises. I called them a living legacy of "busy bees":

Be a responsible legacy ...	to share God's comfort to hurting people.
Be a faithful legacy ...	to bring hope to those in despair. With God no situation is hopeless – not even when we face death!
Be a fearless legacy ...	to stand up for Jesus, reassured that God will certainly be with me. He will never leave me alone!
Be an unchanging legacy ...	to remain in perfect peace when storms arise. God is in control, even when it doesn't look like it.
Be a passionate legacy ...	to never tire of sharing the purpose of the life, death, resurrection and bodily ascension of Jesus!
Be a prayerful legacy ...	to pray in every circumstance! God responds to prayers in Jesus' name. Prayer changes things for me and

| | everyone around me. Blessings only flow when we pray. |
| Be a loving legacy ... | to share God's love to the world demonstrated through Jesus, bringing joy to the unloved. |

God had laid on my heart a powerful 'living legacy' ideal. I wondered at my ability to fulfil it. Without God's power and anointing in my life I could achieve nothing!

Chapter Twelve

P R S Ministries

Ezekiel 47:9

Everything will live where the water goes.

Washing Up Extraordinaire!

I find it amazing how God can speak so clearly through ordinary things. I was washing up my dishes at the kitchen window, and as I looked out I saw that the upper branches on the towering pear tree in a neighbour's garden were heavily laden with large, luscious pears, but the branches that they hung upon were way out of reach. They were too remote to be any good to anyone up there. What an awful waste of good fruit! There was life and sustenance in that fruit, but it was of no benefit if people could not get near it.

As I stared at this tree God spoke to me: "I don't want you to become like that tree!" Instantly, I saw a picture of my life like a tree producing fruit for the benefit of others. God was going to pour out His power and presence through my life, but I was not to be like this fruit tree - out of reach of people. Instead I was to go through every door of opportunity that He would open. I was not to be afraid. He would certainly go with me!

The words God had spoken to Ezekiel suddenly flooded my mind:

Ezekiel 47:9b
Everything will live where the water goes.

Ezekiel, in his vision, had seen water streaming out from the door of God's tabernacle (Ezekiel 47:1-12). At first the stream was a mere trickle coming out from the gate of the Temple, but as it flowed out it became deeper and deeper until it was deep enough to swim in but too deep to walk through. The river continued to grow as it went, bringing life to everything it touched, even the salty waters of the Dead Sea. It showed that God's power and presence in this river was bringing life to everything it touched – even something as dead and desolate as the Dead Sea!

I knew instantly what God was saying to me. Wherever I would go, He would use me to bring eternal life to others through the proclaiming of the Gospel. God was going to pour out His Spirit on my life like a steady stream of water building up inside of me. His anointing power would increase until His life-changing presence literally poured out of me. This was how the prayer I prayed at Mervyn's death-bed would be answered - a 'double portion' would be given abundantly. I reeled with shock. Tears streamed down my cheeks as I saw this picture. What extraordinary times I have had in my kitchen with God!

Jesus had described that He was the source of life-giving water:

John 7:37-39

Anyone who is thirsty may come to me! Anyone who believes in me may come and drink! For the Scriptures declare, 'Rivers of living water will flow from his heart'.

Jesus was speaking symbolically of the Holy Spirit that would be poured out on His followers. Rivers implied great abundance, benefiting not only believers but also those around them. God said:

Acts 2:18

In those days [now] I will pour out my Spirit even on my servants - men and women alike and they will prophesy.

Prophetic Confirmation

Recently I was at a conference led by Rachel Hickson. Rachel is an internationally respected prayer leader, evangelist and Bible teacher with a widely recognized prophetic gift. She is also an author.

At the conference I purchased two of her books and was delighted to have a brief chat with her as she personally signed them. In one she wrote, "Dear Pamela, let the word which is deep flow out and touch many. You are a carrier of grace and peace and will bless many!"

In the other she wrote, "So never let fear contain you... You are made to break control and set captives free. Carry the words of life... and watch freedom be birthed!"

She had no idea how significant her words were to me. It seemed to be a confirmation of how God wanted to use me in the future. As I pondered over her prophetic words and the picture of blessing I received at my kitchen sink, I saw something very special shining majestically over the rivers of living water: of course, my beautiful Romans 8:28 rainbow of seven promises! Little by little, everything was falling into place in unexpected ways!

Billy Graham Evangelistic Association

Through my involvement in the BGEA training programme for the Emerging Evangelists Institute, I had the opportunity to be part of the Franklin Graham Crusade in Belfast. This part of the programme was the one that inspired and motivated me the most. It opened my heart to the possibilities of being used to preach the Gospel if I submitted my life to God's control. Franklin Graham is the President and Chief Executive Officer of both Samaritan's Purse and the BGEA. In Belfast I will always remember how Franklin said, "The call of God to be an evangelist is not for the fainthearted." His words constantly inspire me when I am in challenging situations.

An Evangelist's Appointment!

The apostle Paul wrote to Timothy:

2 Timothy 1:11
And of this Gospel I was appointed a herald and an apostle and a teacher.

Paul had been chosen and sent by Jesus to preach and teach about God's grace. He constantly lifted up the cross of Jesus and called people to repentance. He was an anointed communicator of the Good News of Jesus. The Holy Spirit worked through him to convict, convince and convert many to belief.

Paul, as a mighty evangelist for Jesus, warned that those that present the Gospel are also 'front-liners' in the battle for truth. As such, they will be under constant attack. He taught of the need to be able to "use the weapons of righteousness [God's word] in the right hand for attack and the left hand for defence" (2 Corinthians 6:7b).

The evangelist's only tool for defence and attack is God's sword: the Word.

Ephesians 6:7b
Take the sword of the Spirit, which is the word of God.

I echo what Paul said:

Acts 20:24

My life is worth nothing to me unless I use it for finishing the work assigned me by the Lord Jesus – the work of telling others the Good News about the wonderful grace of God.

This was Paul's first and foremost priority. It is mine too!

The foreword of my book was written by Reverend Frank Parker who prayed this book into existence. I thank God for putting me under his spiritual influence and godly encouragement. I keep a little poem he sent me on my fridge door. The title is "Don't Quit"; it inspires me to keep pressing on, no matter what comes against me.

PRS Ministries

One day, as I doodled on my notepad, I suddenly saw an acronym - Passionately Restoring Scripture - which matched my initials 'PRS'. The Scripture, "everything will live where the water goes" seemed to fit perfectly with this theme. God's Word, like water, restores and revives that which is desolate and dead, but it not only brings new life - it makes things flourish and grow more abundantly. My heart's desire is to have a ministry and reputation of "passionately restoring a love of Scripture" in the hearts and lives of every person I meet.

God has gradually opened doors of opportunity at different events and enabled me to speak, teach, testify and witness as appropriate. My vision for the future is to hold various PRS Seminars in partnership with churches.

One of the most important aspects of any biblical ministry is prayer, due to the supernatural opposition it will arouse. The Apostle Paul realised that he needed the supportive prayer of God's people. He sought intercessors and prayer partners among the Ephesian Christians who would "pray in the Spirit at all times and on every occasion." He wrote:

Ephesians 6:18-19

Pray for me, that words may be given to me in opening my mouth boldly to proclaim the mystery of the Gospel.

I appreciate and thank God continually for all those who faithfully pray for me.

I love the following Scripture:

Zechariah 4:10

Do not despise these small beginnings, for the Lord rejoices to see the work begin.

The thought that Jesus is rejoicing at the work I am seeking to do for Him fills me with awe and delight.

A definition of love I heard somewhere has remained with me:

Love is...

When you feel any sacrifice for a person is worthwhile,
No risk too great,
No deed too brave.
That's love!

That's how I feel about Jesus!

Life's Rich Tapestry

As I write this, I look through the prayer journal I kept during Mervyn's illness. Even now I can hardly bear to read it. I do not want to remember the miserable times; I want to remember the good times. But God in his grace has sustained and strengthened me so I can glorify Him through life's rich tapestry of:

Good and Bad
   Love and Loss
      Tears and Laughter
         Pain and Comfort
            Joy and Sorrow
               Fear and Courage
                  Trouble and Peace
                     Loneliness and Solace
                        Emptiness and Fulfilment
                           Anger and Acceptance
                              Searching and Contentment
                                 Questions & Answers!

The contrasting emotions seem to highlight the precious moments in my life. They sustain me to live in the present with hope for the future chapter(s) of my life. A song that I wrote before I was bereaved seems more poignant and meaningful now.

Jesus, to you everything I bring.
Jesus, I come to you, your call is on my heart.
Jesus, to you, everything I bring,
Make me all you want me to be.

Jesus, I'll take the cross, its message I'll proclaim.
Jesus, to you, everything I bring.
Not my will, but yours be done

Jesus, increase my faith, when I stand alone for you.
Jesus, to you, everything I bring,
Turn my weakness into your strength.

Jesus, when sorrow comes and there are questions why,
Jesus, to you, everything I bring,
All the things I don't understand.

Jesus, I'll gladly go, seeking the lost for you.
Jesus, to you, everything I bring,

By your grace I'll follow your call.

One thing is crystal clear: as I look back at everything that has happened to me since I started my journey with God, I can truly say, as the apostle Paul did:

Philippians 1: 12
I want you to know, my dear brothers and sisters, that everything that has happened to me here has helped to spread the Good News.

In the light of eternity, isn't that all that really matters?

Transformed By Grace

As I end this book, it is not the end of God's work in my life. It is the beginning of a new chapter. It reminds me of one of the final things Mervyn said to me just before he died: "Our time together was just one chapter in life's book. You have more chapters to come. Enjoy them!"

Once I was a caterpillar, but now I am a butterfly! That is an apt description of my life. A butterfly emerges from its dark cocoon with a struggle as it develops, but it is experiencing the most profound changes. The entire body of the larva is dismembered and reassembled. Something amazing is happening. At the right time it emerges transformed into a beautiful butterfly. It is just another example of nature's miracles and mysteries.

This insignificant caterpillar, by the grace of God, has emerged from its dark cocoon of pain and sorrow. It has been transformed by God's grace into a beautiful butterfly. It finds to its delight that it can fly. It is airborne at last. Now, as His 'masterpiece and miracle', the possibilities are limitless!

I know that there will be plenty of turbulence in the days ahead as I am going to be a butterfly that is determined to fly high, but with Jesus at my controls and my Romans 8:28 rainbow of promises overhead, what have I to fear?

This little butterfly intends to trust God and, in the words of Mervyn, 'enjoy' the flight!

Isaiah 40:31
Those who trust in the Lord will find new strength.
They will soar high on wings like eagles.
They will run and not grow weary.
They will walk and not faint.

Contact the author:

Email: pamela-ruth@prsministries.com
Website: prsministries.com

Contact Compassion:

Compassion UK
43 High Street
Weybridge
Surrey
KT13 8BB

Phone: 01932-836490
Email: info@compassionuk.org
Web: www.compassion.org

Similar Books from the Publisher

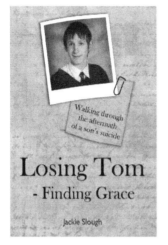

Written as a journal it is an honest and intimate revelation of one woman's ability to cope with the unexpected suicide of her teenage son.

Tom was a deep-thinking and creative young man, and an active Christian. How can a young Christian commit suicide? How can a parent not feel condemned? What goes through the minds of people in these circumstances? Excerpts from Tom's Diary are included.

You will find it difficult to put this book down. As you read through the emotional honesty of this narrative you will wonder at God's amazing grace.

"Death has its own diary. Sometimes it sends its visitor's card in advance; at other times it turns up unexpectedly and unannounced. Death's visits often seem random, meaningless and, in the minds of many, unjust. Invariably, however, those left behind find themselves grappling with a miscellany of emotions and thoughts which have to be worked through."

In this book Geoff Treasure offers hope, comfort and advice to those who are grieving the loss of a loved one, with sensitivity and understanding.

Books available from **www.onwardsandupwards.org**